To Elaine
May this book
bless you & j
you wisdom.
Apostle [illegible]
12-27-01

# Acknowledgements

I would like to thank my beloved wife, Darlene, the reflection of glory and my best friend. Thanks for being virtuous and full of love.

Thanks to Bishop Skip Horton for your vision of unity and your love of the brethren. Thanks to Dr. Miles Monroe for your inspiring words of wisdom and your boldness to speak by revelation, the "deeper things of God."

Thanks to my friend Bishop T.N. Josiah, a true man of God, for your kindness, your love, and for reflecting the true image and brightness of the glory of God.

Thanks to Bishop Charles E. Blake for your anointing and your faithfulness to be a jewel to the city and a light to the world.

# Behold The Woman


First Printing 2001
All scripture Quotations are taken from the King James/ New International Version of the Holy Bible unless otherwise noted.



ISBN 09704127-4-6
Published By:
Anointed Publishing
2940 W. Lincoln Ave.# D410
Anaheim, Ca. 92801
(562) 918-0950

# Introduction

It is reported in today's statistics that one out of every three women have been mentally, physically and sexually abused. This mindset started in the Garden of Eden, when sin came into the world and gave license to these and many other demonic activities, to operate in the earth realm. These attitudes of corrupt behavior have continued its plight until now. In this new millennium, we are faced with the alarming rate of women who also abuse men and children. This too is reported in epidemic proportions. The effects of sin has moved every foundation off course.

***"They know not, neither will they understand; they walk on in darkness: all the foundations of the earth are out of course." [Ps. 82:5]***

The level of ignorance in man concerning the glory of God is not by accident, but is by design of the devil. As long as man is ignorant of his own glory and of the glory of God, he will abuse himself and the woman who was created to "***help***" him. It is written;

***"But the natural man receiveth not the things of the Spirit of God: for they are foolishness unto him: neither can he know them, because they are spiritually discerned." [1 Cor. 2:14-15]***

While Satan works hard to keep men and women ignorant of who they *really* are, and the glory that is in them, his ultimate goal is to destroy them. Ignorance is a destroyer of the mind. He will do anything to keep men and women from the knowledge of God, which will reveal their true identity.

***"In whom the god of this world hath blinded the minds of them which believe not, lest the light of the glorious gospel of Christ, who is the image of God, should shine unto them." [2 Cor. 4:4]***

Thanks to God who never leaves us comfortless, we no longer have to suffer this ignorance. God sent us some new help, incorruptible, infallible, untouchable by sin, holy, just and righteous. The Lord Of Glory, King Jesus Christ! Amen!

***"And ye shall know the truth, and the truth shall make you free." [John 8:32]***

This book uncovers and reveals the truth about the *divine* purpose of the woman. It is a must for every marriage, and every man and woman who may be contemplating marriage. **Every man should, *BEHOLD THE WOMAN!***

# Dedications

*This book is dedicated to my wife Darlene, my heartbeat in the morning, my sunshine, my glory and my victory. I love you with the love that surpass knowledge. You propel my altitude to new heights, and with your kiss you assure my heart that I am safely in love. You are awesome! Thank you for your tolerance of an Apostle.*

*To my mother Joyce Wallace, who have always been a pillar of strength and good advice, A virtuous woman of God. Thanks for your love and prayers. All the love of a son.*

*To all the women of God who have blessed the world with virtue and life. You are a wonder to behold, God's gift to man, so I am told, you were created with power, to be a divine helper for the hour.*

~

***"Oh that my words were now written! oh that they were printed in a book!***

***That they were graven with an iron pen and lead in the rock for ever!***

***For I know that my redeemer liveth, and that he shall stand at the latter day upon the earth:"***
***[Job 19:23-26]***

# Contents

# Acknowledgements

*To my mother in law Dale Clinton for your virtuous wisdom and your beautiful poise, your joy and laughter adds blessings to my blessings. Thank you for being the virtuous woman of God and the bond of love.*

*To all the Superwomen, who have raised the children, guided the house, carried the family through thick and thin, through sickness and health, through good times and bad times, who always pressed for the mark for the prize of the high calling of God. You are God's anointed Superwomen who have held the whole world together with your virtue! Thank you for your many wonderful gifts and virtue. You are the victory and God's gift to men! Thank you for your unspeakable gifts.*

*To all the women who are suffering, or have suffered unhappiness in a marital relationship. You are misunderstood, and mistaken for the enemy, but you are the apple of God's eye and a blessing to behold. You are more than what they think, and your virtue will not go unrecognized. Thank you for not giving up on pressing forward, looking to God for help in times of need. Moving from faith to faith, from disaster to victory, from glory to glory. You are destined to meet God's reality of blessings for your life. Thank you for your virtue!*

# Chapter One

## God's Gift To Man

***House and riches are the inheritance of fathers: and a prudent wife is from the Lord. [Prov. 19:14]***

Man is recipient of a great blessing called, "woman." She was created by God, for man. FOR THE MAN, BECAUSE MAN HAD NO COMPANION FOR HIMSELF. Man had no other species after *his* kind. God made man after *His* kind, or after His likeness. God's purpose for her creation was to fulfill man's loneliness, and to help him to replenish the earth through childbearing.

***"So God created man in his own image, in the image of God created he him; male and female created he them." [Gen. 1:27]***

God created the woman and presented her to the man as a gift and to see what he would name her.

***"And the LORD God caused a deep sleep to fall upon Adam and he slept: and he took one of his ribs, and closed up the flesh instead thereof; And the rib, which the LORD God had taken from man, made he a woman, and brought her unto the man. And Adam***

*said, This is now bone of my bones, and flesh of my flesh: she shall be called Woman, because she was taken out of Man." [Gen. 2:21-23]*

**The woman is in deed a gift from God to man. She is designed to be HIS helper by creation. She helps the man complete the reflection of the image and glory of God.**

God created the woman as a blessing to the man, and made her pleasing to his sight. In the beginning man was pleased with the woman in every way. She helped the man reflect the glory of God, by virtue of all the intricate details of power that God placed in her for the man. She also, inherently reflected man's emotions and desires, because she was taken out of the man. The woman was created as an asset to the man, unique in every way.

Before the fall, Adam and Eve shared in direct reflection of God's glory, and their fellowship was in the presence of God, but after the fall she could only reflected *man's* glory, because sin had broken the process of God's imaging towards man.

***"But your iniquities have separated between you and your God, and your sins have hid his face from***

***you, that he will not hear." [Isa. 59:2]***

Before the fall, she was a virgin, chaste, and pure, to reflect the pure reflection of the image and glory of God, as did the man. Notice after the fall, that the man begot children after his *own* likeness and image, which had become corrupted by sin and death.

***"Wherefore, as by one man sin entered into the world, and death by sin; and so death passed upon all men, for that all have sinned:" [Rom. 5:9]***

***"And Adam lived an hundred and thirty years, and begat a son in his own likeness, after his image; and called his name Seth:" [Gen. 5:3]***

Before Eve was taken out of man, she inherently received, by virtue of being a part of Adam's being, the beginning of the image and glory of God. The glory which man had before Eve was created, was only the beginning of a process. Man, who had dominion over the earth, was also a partaker in the creation process by naming all the animals. It was, in a real since, "Adam's world." The fullness of God's glory was not revealed until Eve was created, but the imaging process had just begun, because the woman was the physical completion of the creation of man, not a separate entity, but a component of the man, another part of his body, like his arm or leg. Adam understood who, and what she was.

***"And Adam said, This is now bone of my bones, and flesh of my flesh: she shall be called Woman, because she was taken out of Man." Therefore shall a man leave his father and his mother, and shall cleave unto his wife: and they shall be one flesh." [Gen. 2:23-24]***

In the day that God created Adam he also created Eve, who was inside of Adam, and God saw them as one man, and called their name *Adam.*

***"Male and female created he them; and blessed them, and called their name Adam, in the day when they were created." [Gen. 5:2]***

When the woman was revealed to man, they both lived in harmony with God for an undisclosed amount of time, because they were sustained by the tree of life. Adam was pleased with this unspeakably beautiful gift. A perfect helper and companion, a friend, fulfilling all his loneliness. She could talk, walk, reason, dialog, and understand God's commands. They were very happy in the paradise of God called "the Garden." In it was everything that man needed for life. But there was also in the garden the potential of death, which God had warned the man not to partake of. The innocence of Adam and Eve was disrupted by the subtlety of the devil, who took the form of a beautiful upright walking creature who could also talk, called a serpent. The woman was lured into transgression by cunning trickery and was deceived. Adam however, was not deceived, but yet he was a partaker of the same transgression.

***"And the serpent said unto the woman, Ye shall not surely die: For God doth know that in the day ye eat thereof, then your eyes shall be opened, and ye shall be as gods, knowing good and evil. And when the woman saw that the tree was good for food, and that it was pleasant to the eyes, and a tree to be desired to make one wise, she took of the fruit thereof, and did eat, and gave also unto her husband with her; and he did eat." [Gen. 3:4-6]***

This is an intriguing verse of scripture. But let's take a deeper look. First we see a picture here of the serpent throwing out the trap of temptation through the use of lies. What was the lie? The subtlety of the lie was camouflaged with part of the truth, as is most lies. The lie was, *"ye shall not surely die."* This put the woman at ease, and reduced the risk factor. Then the devil gave her some truth to mix with the lie, and further enticed her with the optical illusions (lust of the eyes) of the benefits of eating from the tree. ***"For God doth know that in the day ye eat thereof, then your eyes shall be opened, and ye shall be as gods, knowing good***

***and evil."*** This portion was the bait that allured her to analyze, reason, doubt, and ultimately believe the lie. Now we must understand that although the woman had a mind and will of her own to obey or disobey, she was also taken from within the man. She was an embodiment of his inner desires and emotions. She had her husband in mind when she took of the tree. It was not just a self motivated act of wanting to gain wisdom outside of the knowledge of Adam, but she was thinking about how the tree could benefit her and how she could please her husband. Adam was not somewhere sleeping, he was there with his wife, no doubt, watching her talk to the serpent.

***"And when the woman saw that the tree was good for food, and that it was pleasant to the eyes, and a tree to be desired to make one wise, she took of the fruit thereof, and did eat, and gave also unto her husband with her; and he did eat." [Gen. 3:6]***

First she reasoned and analyzed in her mind, and assessed that the tree *was* good for sustenance. Secondly, she saw that it looked harmless, and ripe, ready to be harvested. Then thirdly she thought that by doing this it would make her husband happy and wise. So she ate of the tree. **Notice, she gave also unto her husband with her; and he did eat. I am convinced**

**that she was acting out *his* inner desires.** Notice he did not rebuke her, he did not resist in any way her gift from the tree. He did not remind her of the commandment of God. He did what he desired to do, that is, to eat of the tree. He saw that she did not immediately die, after she had eaten of the tree, so he was indirectly deceived by the same lie told to him through the woman. ***"Thou shall not surely die." It is good for food, and besides that, it will make us wise!*** So Adam disregarded the commandment of God and listened to his wife. ***"And unto Adam he said, BECAUSE THOU HAST HEARKENED UNTO THE VOICE OF THY WIFE, and hast eaten of the tree, of which I commanded thee, saying, Thou shalt not eat of it: cursed is the ground for thy sake; in sorrow shalt thou eat of it all the days of thy life;" [Gen. 3:17]***

Adam obeyed a lie, as well as the woman, and he *did* eat. The scripture says that Adam was not deceived, but the woman being deceived was in the transgression.

***"For Adam was first formed, then Eve. And Adam was not deceived, but the woman being deceived was in the transgression." [1 Tim. 2:13-14]***

This simply implies that Adam was not deceived in his obedience to a lie or *first* to transgress. The Greek word for *deceived* is rendered ***apatao***: which suggests that he was not *diluted.* He was willfully disobedient to God's command, because he did what he desired to do, (eat of the tree). But the woman was ***exapatao*** ; (that is, to seduce wholly:) was completely and wholly deceived.

Although Adam may have desired to eat of the tree, he was not first to do so. The woman ate of the tree first, and lost her glory, and her fellowship with God was broken.

***"But your iniquities have separated between you and your God, and your sins have hid his face from you, that he will not hear." [Isa. 59:2]***

Her features changed and her brilliance (luminosity) departed. Adam knew that she would surely die!

***"When thou with rebukes dost correct man for iniquity, thou makest his beauty to consume away like a moth: surely every man is vanity. Selah." [Ps. 39:11]***

She lost the *Shekinah Glory* which both her and Adam were wrapped in before the fall, as the second man Jesus received on the mount of transfiguration.

***"And his raiment became shining, exceeding white as snow; so as no fuller on earth can white them." [Mark 9:3-4]***

Adam's plan was to attempt to redeem her by

becoming one with her through the same transgression. He saw that she had lost her light and that the glory of God did not shine on her any longer. Out of disobedience he partook of the forbidden fruit to redeem his wife from her dismay. This was not an act of ignorance, but of compassion for his wife.

This was a shadow and a figure of things to come. It was a picture of what Jesus, "the second Adam," would do for His wife, the church.

***"For he hath made him to be sin for us, who knew no sin; that we might be made the righteousness of God in him." [2 Cor. 5:21]***

He saw that his wife (the Church) was dismayed and marred with spot and blemishes. So He said, I will redeem her and cleanse her, and present her to myself as my wife without spot, and I will present her faultless before my presence with exceeding joy.

***"Husbands, love your wives, even as Christ also loved the church, and gave himself for it; That he might sanctify and cleanse it with the washing of water by the word, That he might present it to himself a glorious church, not having spot, or wrinkle, or any such thing; but that it should be holy and without***

***blemish." [Eph. 5:25-28]***

When the woman was taken out of the man, God took a rib from his flesh and closed up the flesh thereof. When the second Adam was in process of redeeming His wife while on the cross, a spear was thrust into His side, to signify that the rib could now come back into her rightful place in glory. His wife could now be cleansed and sanctified for redemption. Out of His side came forth blood and water. The blood for her redemption and the water for her sanctification.

***"But one of the soldiers with a spear pierced his side, and forthwith came there out blood and water." [John 19:34]***

The blood, the water, and the spirit are three witnesses at the reuniting of the second Adam and his wife.

***"And there are three that bear witness in earth, the spirit, and the water, and the blood: and these three agree in one." [1 John 5:8]***

***"By the which will we are sanctified through the offering of the body of Jesus Christ once for all." [Heb. 10:10]***

## Sin's administration and affects

The results of this deception was a universal catastrophe. It ushered in death, it distorted the universe, every foundation was out of course. It affected the animals also. They became vicious, and began to eat meat instead of herbs and vegetation which God had commanded in their creation.

***"And to every beast of the earth, and to every fowl of the air, and to every thing that creepeth upon the earth, wherein there is life, I have given every green herb for meat: and it was so." [Gen. 1:31]***

The wolf, who was accustomed to grazing with the lamb, would now attack, and eat the lamb by virtue of his very nature, which was now altered.

***"The wolf and the lamb shall feed together, and the lion shall eat straw like the bullock: and dust shall be the serpent's meat. They shall not hurt nor destroy in all my holy mountain, saith the LORD." [Isa. 65:25-66:1]***

All the elements in the universe of man was affected by sin. The man was now to till the earth which was cursed and unyielding [hard labor] for his bread, whereas before, God provided everything he needed to sustain his life, forever, in the garden, and the man's only job was to dress and maintain the garden. The woman was now to bring forth life with pain and sorrow, whereas before, there was no such thing as pain nor sorrow. She would now be limited to reflect only man's glory, and her desires to reflect the glory of God, will be now towards her husband, and he shall rule over her.

***"Unto the woman he said, I will greatly multiply thy sorrow and thy conception; in sorrow thou shalt bring forth children; and thy desire shall be to thy husband, and he shall rule over thee." [Gen. 3:16]***

The woman whom God created, was altered in her thinking, and in her perfection to be a blessing and a helper. She was now cursed to suffer pain, and sorrow. Sin became king over mankind as a result of her actions. The *Gift* of God was distorted by the deception of the devil, and the administration of sin. The administration of sin appointed all unrighteousness of the enemy. With it came pain, sorrow, sickness, disease, age, corruption or waste, lies, death, and blood (the life of the *flesh* was now in the blood, whereas, before sin came, the life of the flesh was sustained by every Word of God). That is why the scripture says, that "***man shall not live by bread alone but by every word that proceed out of the mouth of God." [Matt. 4:4]***

Blood circulation represents corruption and waste. It is not subject to eternal life.

***"Now this I say brethren, that flesh and blood***

***cannot enter the kingdom of God; neither doth corruption inherit incorruption." [1 Cor. 15:50]***

The woman is reminded of the reality of this corruption every month in her menstruation cycle. This was part of the curse which came with sin's administration.

In Christ we are restored in the fellowship of everlasting life by obeying every Word of God. However, our bodies have not yet been redeemed and is yet subject to time, sin and death.

***"O wretched man that I am! who shall deliver me from the body of this death? I thank God through Jesus Christ our Lord. So then with the mind I myself serve the law of God; but with the flesh the law of sin." [Rom. 7:24-25]***

***"For we know that the whole creation groaneth and travaileth in pain together until now. And not only they, but ourselves also, which have the firstfruits of the Spirit, even we ourselves groan within ourselves, waiting for the adoption, to wit, the redemption of our body." [Rom. 8:22-23]***

In Christ we receive a new body that is not subject to corruption, death, or blood, but it will once again be sustained by the Word of God according to the original design.

*"They shall hunger no more, neither thirst any more; neither shall the sun light on them, nor any heat. For the Lamb which is in the midst of the throne shall feed them, and shall lead them unto living fountains of waters: and God shall wipe away all tears from their eyes." [Rev. 7:16-17]*

*"For this corruptible must put on incorruption, and this mortal must put on immortality. So when this corruptible shall have put on incorruption, and this mortal shall have put on immortality, then shall be brought to pass the saying that is written, Death is swallowed up in victory." [1 Cor. 15:53-54]*

That which was lost through the acceptance of one lie told in the garden (***"Thou shall not surely die"***), was restored through the acceptance of one *Truth* which is Christ Jesus our Lord. ***[John 14:6-7] [Rom. 5:18-19]***

*"Therefore as by the offence of one judgment came upon all men to condemnation; even so by the righteousness of one the free gift came upon all men unto justification of life. For as by one man's disobedience many were made sinners, so by the obedience of one shall many be made righteous." [Rom. 5:18-19]*

# Chapter Two

## Behold The Woman

***"Whoso findeth a wife findeth a good thing, and obtaineth favour of the LORD." [Prov. 18:22]***

A jeweler hurried for work one morning, when on his way to work his car began to stall. It finally came to a stop, directly in the front of the city dump. He went in to use the phone, but no one was at the front desk. He wondered out back where the garbage trucks were hard at work dumping refuse into a heap of rubble. The jeweler approached the trucks to ask for help, but as he got close to the pile of garbage he noticed a large egg shaped chunk of rock. He immediately reached into the horrible smelling garbage and pulled the rock out from the rubble. The man in the garbage truck yelled, "hey, what are you doing?" The jeweler replied, "I found this rock in the garbage, may I keep it?" The man in the garbage truck looked at the jeweler and said sarcastically, "you can have all the rocks in this dump if you like, old kook, now get out of the yard before you get hurt." The jeweler said, "thank you," as he walked briskly towards the front of the building to his car. He scrambled around for his keys to his car. Finally he opened the car door and quickly reached into his glove compartment and pulled out some jeweler's tools. He nervously examined the huge chunk of stinking rock and discovered it was an uncut diamond!

**When a man does not know the value of a woman, he will discard her into the garbage heap. He will misuse her, and abuse her by virtue of ignorance. If he discerns her value, he will, just as the jeweler did, cherish her, protect her, put her in a safe place, and love her as he loves and values his own body. (whom she is in a figure.)**

***"So ought men to love their wives as their own bodies. He that loveth his wife loveth himself. For no man ever yet hated his own flesh; but nourisheth and cherisheth it, even as the Lord the church: For we are members of his body, of his flesh, and of his bones. For this cause shall a man leave his father and mother, and shall be joined unto his wife, and they two shall be one flesh. This is a great mystery: but I speak concerning Christ and the church. Nevertheless let every one of you in particular so love his wife even as himself; and the wife see that she reverence her husband." [Eph. 5:28-6:1]*** One man's ignorance became another man's treasure. The jeweler, immediately, upon seeing the rock, perceived it's value. **You can not know the value of a thing unless you know *what* it is.** The same rock was perceived by all else as a worthless chunk of rock, but to the jeweler, it was precious, because he realized *what* it was. Today most men do not seem to have a clue who or what the woman is! So the woman is therefore used by the man for something other than the intended design. Like a makeshift tool may be misused, so is the woman, misused by virtue of ignorance of *what* she is and *who* she is.

I remember many times in my life where I had to use something as a makeshift tool, to get the job done, until I found out how efficient the proper tools were for the job. There were times when I tried using a shoe to drive a nail in the wall. It drove the nail, but the shoe was not fit for wearing anymore. I tried using a sharp knife for a screwdriver. The tip of the knife would always bend or break, because it was not designed to do what a screwdriver was designed for.

When a woman is misused she may lose her efficiency for glory and true imaging and become unfruitful. She then becomes a distortion of the truth. **Some women think that the length of time spent in a marriage, equals success. She may be in a marriage for seventeen years, but only living as a shoe!** Or functioning according to the ignorance of what the world thinks she ought to be. Being married for long lengths of time is good, if it is functioning in the capacity of the glory of God, for which it was designed.

Many women have told me, after briefly browsing my first book, *"How To Steer Clear Of A Bozo and Stay Away From The Circus,"* "This book is not for me, I've been married for sixteen years." Others have commented "I wish you had written this book five years ago!" Many women have become comfortable with the idea of just being married, even if they are in a miserable state of mind. Some women have lived in dysfunctional marriages for so long, they will settle for what little they can get from their husbands, and count their dysfunctions as *normal.*

Many *women* today have lost focus on who they are, and what they are, by reason of believing the lies or revisions made by each generation. Satan hates the woman! The woman is a threat to his kingdom, because she can produce an army, having the power to multiply.

***"And I will put enmity between thee and the woman, and between thy seed and her seed; it shall bruise thy head, and thou shalt bruise his heel." [Gen. 3:15]***

Years of social, psychological and spiritual abuse

of the woman, have concealed the truth about her original purpose.

In the beginning, when the woman was created, Adam was asleep. However, Satan was not! He was aware of the power that God gave to the woman. She was given the awesome power of *dunamis and exousia which gave her license to have audience with God. She was* connected to God for constant flow of integrity and strength. When a virtuous woman petition God for help He hears her and answer. Because she is connected and anointed for help.

*(exousia (ex-oo-see'-ah); (in the sense of ability); privilege, force, capacity, competency, freedom, or mastery (concretely, magistrate, superhuman, potentate, token of control), delegated influence:)*

*dunamis (doo'-nam-is); from force (literally or figuratively); specially, miraculous power (usually by implication, a miracle itself):*

Satan knew that this "*virtue power*" was created to magnify and reflect the image and "glory likeness" of God in man, and that it was given to the woman to help the man fulfill that purpose.

***"Neither was the man created for the woman; but***

***the woman for the man. For this cause ought the woman to have power on her head because of the angels." [1 Cor. 11:9-10]***

This was symbolic of her spiritual function, to be in willful subjection to her head, or husband in a the public assembly. To wear a veil was to illustrate her subordination to his authority. The angels are always present in the congregation, standing also in the presence of God on our behalf.

***"Take heed that ye despise not one of these little ones; for I say unto you, That in heaven their angels do always behold the face of my Father which is in heaven."[ Matt. 18:10]***

In the spirit this power signifies the woman's authority, not over the man, but for the man, to help him in reflecting the image of God by honor.

Satan knew also, that if this power was used negatively it could destroy the man. Satan saw an opportunity to capture this power over men. He is always seeking to overthrow God's plan of imaging through attempting to steal and entice or bribe men to obtain the power that God gave Adam and Eve before the fall. This power of authority and dominion was given to Adam and the virtue to Eve. The second Adam had both the Authority, Dominion of the first Adam and the Virtue of the woman, because He had no sin. Satan studies man to see how he can steal that power from men to destroy them.

***"And when Simon saw that through laying on of the apostles' hands the Holy Ghost was given, he offered them money, Saying, Give me also this power, that on whomsoever I lay hands, he may receive the Holy Ghost." [Acts 8:18-19]***

***"And the devil, taking him up into an high mountain, shewed unto him all the kingdoms of the world in a moment of time. And the devil said unto him, All this power will I give thee, and the glory of them: for that is delivered unto me; and to whomsoever I will I give it.***

***If thou therefore wilt worship me, all shall be thine." [Luke 4:5-7]***

So he devised his plan of deception to overthrow the whole world through obtaining the *virtue power* of the woman and the *exousia* authority of the man, which God gave them to have *DOMINION* or power and authority over everything that have breath, or every living thing, including the devil.

***"And God blessed them, and God said unto them,***

*Be fruitful, and multiply, and replenish the earth, and subdue it: and have dominion over the fish of the sea, and over the fowl of the air, and over every living thing that moveth upon the earth." [Gen. 1:28-29]*

*"And the great dragon was cast out, that old serpent, called the Devil, and Satan, which deceiveth the whole world: he was cast out into the earth, and his angels were cast out with him." [Rev. 12:9]*

**Sin is a manifestation of virtue (dunamis and exousia) working in reverse. Reverse virtue is, virtue that is disconnected from God, and it has no integrity for light, but only for darkness. That is, to steal kill and destroy. What ever is in reverse is perverse.** The devil obtained the title "god of this world," and the prince of the power or *exousia* of the air, or everything that has breath, after seducing the woman of her *virtue power* and the man of his *exousia* authority.

*"Wherein in time past ye walked according to the course of this world, according to the prince of the power of the air, the spirit that now worketh in the children of disobedience:" [Eph. 2:2]*

The *virtue power* from the woman, and the *exousia authority* from the man, was given to the devil through the disobedience of Adam and the deception of Eve.

This power was then used in reverse or darkness, and produced sickness, disease, poverty, death, and hell (the place of torment made for the devil).

***"Forasmuch then as the children are partakers of flesh and blood, He also Himself likewise took part of the same; that through death He might destroy Him that had the power of death, that is, the devil;" [Heb. 2:14]***

***"And the devil said unto him, All this power will I give thee, and the glory of them: for that is delivered unto me; and to whomsoever I will I give it. [Luke 4:6]***

This power over man was broken and destroyed through our Lord Jesus Christ who paid the price for our deliverance from the effects of reverse virtue, and exousia, which is sin. Since death was the ultimate effect of sin, Jesus had to overcome death to obtain power over the devil's claim to dominion over the earth.

***"I am he that liveth, and was dead; and, behold, I am alive for evermore, Amen; and have the keys of hell and of death." [Rev. 1:18]***

Now that Jesus has taken this power back, the devil is rendered powerless over the sons of God. The power of God is restored unto us in light or righteousness.

*"Not by works of righteousness which we have done, but according to his mercy he saved us, by the washing of regeneration, and renewing of the Holy Ghost;*

*Which he shed on us abundantly through Jesus Christ our Saviour; That being justified by his grace, we should be made heirs according to the hope of eternal life."*

This power was restored to us by Jesus our Lord and our God, and we now have power again, over the devil.

*"And he said unto them, I beheld Satan as lightning fall from heaven." "Behold, I give unto you power to tread on serpents and scorpions, and over all the power of the enemy: and nothing shall by any means hurt you." [Luke 10:18-19]*

*"For God, who commanded the light to shine out of darkness, hath shined in our hearts, to give the light of the knowledge of the glory of God in the face of Jesus Christ. But we have this treasure in earthen vessels, that the excellency of the power may be of God, and not of us." [2 Cor. 4:6-7]*

## Lies and Slander Wars Against Confidence

***"Cast not away therefore your confidence, which hath great recompence of reward. For ye have need of patience, that, after ye have done the will of God, ye might receive the promise." [Heb. 10:35-36]***

Some lies used by Satan through men concerning the woman, may sound like this; you are just for sex, you are second class, You are good for nothing, you do not look as good as the next woman. You are too fat, or too skinny, you talk too much, or not enough. Your hair is not long enough. What happened to the shape you had before the three kids? This kind of abuse does not stop at the secular world, but it is also evident in the churches today, among those who are "saved." You may hear things like; The bible said, you can not teach, you can not preach, you can not wear jewelry, you can not paint your toes, you can not, wear make up, you can not wear pants, you cannot, you cannot, you cannot! You pray too long or you don't pray enough, you're not as spiritual as I thought you were before we got married!

These lies are told to keep you off balance, out of focus, and faithless. If your confidence in God is shaken, your virtue can not work effectually. It is like trying to blow a sweet melody on a flute that has rusted keys. The song will be somewhat distorted, because *all* the keys must work together to produce the perfect sound.

Likewise when lies ruin your confidence it hinders your spiritual keys of faith towards God. **Faith is necessary for virtue.** Do not fall for these lies about who you are and what you are.

**Keep your self esteem no matter what the devil placed in your past.**

Because you've been redeemed, washed, sanctified, justified, renewed, transformed, mortified, and glorified in the name of Jesus! And the devil don't like it!

Lost self esteem will cause a woman to pawn her virtue to the devil. She will lower her moral and spiritual standards to fulfill her need for love, for which she was designed to reflect. Confidence and self esteem, that is, acknowledging who, and what you are, activates your anointing, and you become the virtuous woman that God made you. Stir up that which is in you, which you have received of God for help!

***"That the communication of thy faith may become effectual by the acknowledging of every good thing***

***which is in you in Christ Jesus." [ Philem. 6]***

Each generation, after the fall of man, had its own revisions of the original design. So that, the woman that we see in the *world* today, is not the woman in the original design. The devil, has distorted the true image of reflection, to become evil or perverted.

Some women are deceived to think that the use of sexual pleasures can build their self esteem. Sex have become an intricate part of the misuse and abuse of the design and function of the woman. Sexual attraction is not a taboo subject to those for which it was designed. It is, however, only a small part of the vast glory that is placed in every woman that God created. **Sex is designed for marriage, and marriage is designed for loves fulfillment. It reflects a picture of the pleasures we have in the presence of God when we love Him.**

***"Thou wilt shew me the path of life: in thy presence is fulness of joy; at thy right hand there are pleasures for evermore." [Ps. 16:11-17:1]***

**It confirms the oness and intimacy that the *head* enjoys with the *body*.**

***"For we are members of his body, of his flesh, and of his bones." [Eph. 5:30]***

*"For this cause shall a man leave his father and mother, and shall be joined unto his wife, and they two shall be one flesh. This is a great mystery: but I speak concerning Christ and the church." [Eph. 5:31-32]*

**There are physical and spiritual treasures inside of the woman.** She may not know that she has these gifts, and treasures, but they were placed in her at the time of her creation. This knowledge of the glory of God was concealed, when sin came into the world, and Satan blinded the mind, blocking the entrance of light and the knowledge of the glory of God. But it is revealed through Christ and restored unto us by His Spirit.

*"In whom the god of this world hath blinded the minds of them which believe not, lest the light of the glorious gospel of Christ, who is the image of God, should shine unto them." [ 2 Cor. 4: 4]*

*"For God, who commanded the light to shine out of darkness, hath shined in our hearts, to give the light of the knowledge of the glory of God in the face of Jesus Christ." [2 Cor. 4:7]*

*"The entrance of thy words giveth light; it giveth understanding unto the simple." [Ps. 119:130]*

This great treasure was given to us by His Spirit. So, through Him we may *know* the things freely given to us by God.

***"Now we have received, not the spirit of the world, but the spirit which is of God; that we might know the things that are freely given to us of God." [1 Cor. 2:12]***

***"But we have this treasure in earthen vessels, that the excellency of the power may be of God, and not of us." [2 Cor. 4:7]***

In Christ, a man is restored into fellowship with God, and he reflects the true image and likeness of God by conforming to the image of Christ through obedience to the Word of God.

***"But we all, with open face beholding as in a glass the glory of the Lord, are changed into the same image from glory to glory, even as by the Spirit of the Lord." [2 Cor. 3:18]***

The woman is restored into her place of anointing. She was created to be virtuous. She has hidden wisdom and resources inside her to build the house (spiritual house).

***"Every wise woman buildeth her house: but the foolish plucketh it down with her hands." [Prov. 14:1]***

***"Through wisdom is an house builded; and by understanding it is established: And by knowledge shall the chambers be filled with all precious and pleasant riches. [Prov. 24:3-4]***

When a woman surrenders to God by faith in Christ Jesus, she then conforms to His image by transformation into the original design. She becomes a virtuous woman by reflecting the image and glory of God through the man.

## Words can affect Virtue

A negative word from a husband's mouth can destroy a wife's fruitfulness. What a wife *hears,* she reflects. A man who wants his wife to be virtuous, must speak virtue to her, and she will multiply the honor back to him and God is glorified. When a man honors God, by walking in the fear of the LORD, his wife receives the reflection of that fear and honor towards God, and she *magnifies* it through her submission to her husband and her faith towards God, thus, God himself is glorified, and the entire family is blessed of God.

***"Blessed is every one that feareth the LORD; that walketh in his ways. For thou shalt eat the labour of***

***thine hands: happy shalt thou be, and it shall be well with thee. Thy wife shall be as a fruitful vine by the sides of thine house: thy children like olive plants round about thy table. Behold, that thus shall the man be blessed that feareth the LORD" [Ps. 128:1-4]***

A man must cultivate his wife with life, health, and peace, by his words.

***"Pleasant words are as an honeycomb, sweet to the soul, and health to the bones." [Prov. 16:24]***

Speak nothing but positive things to her spirit. Build her up mentally, by reminding her how intelligent she is, and how much you appreciate her intelligence. Never tear her down with your mouth concerning her physical makeup. **A man has power over the body of his wife.** Encourage your wife! If she is in good physical shape, **love her,** if she is out of shape, **love her,** remind her how beautiful she is at all times, whether she meets your *fantasy* standards or not. Build her up spiritually by allowing her to pray *for* you and *with* you. Give her place in the things of God by listening to her. Honor her and she will bless you!

**A man ministers to his wife through the abundance of a quality ear.** Listen to her complaints, listen to her joys, her revelations, her spiritual appetite, her dreams, her likes, dislikes and her sexual pleasures. **Remember your wife will incubate, analyze, multiply and magnify what you give. Whatever you project, she reflects. Your words can increase your favor with God or hinder your prayers.**

***"Likewise, ye husbands, dwell with them according to knowledge, giving honour unto the wife, as unto the weaker vessel, and as being heirs together of the grace of life; that your prayers be not hindered." [1 Peter 3:7]***

**When a man continues to talk negative to his wife, he is building a spiritual time bomb!**

Everything he says is being kept in incubation to be analyzed, multiplied and magnified, for use at some later and unexpected date. When a man's negative put downs and words, come back to him through the mouth of the woman, which she has now incubated, analyzed, multiplied and magnified, they will have the power to render him impotent! (*powerless*) A woman's words can destroy a man's spiritual experience, or can add life to his life.

***"Death and life are in the power of the tongue: and they that love it shall eat the fruit thereof." [Prov. 18:21]***

**Don't be hung by the tongue**

# Chapter Three

## Spiritual Abuse

Some preachers have used the bible erroneously, to ignorantly justify their spiritual abuse of women. Some are so dogmatic in this abuse that they vehemently oppose women standing or sitting in the pulpit. How carnal! The pulpit is symbolic for the holy place of God and His sanctuary. The pulpit is made of wood, and nails, and brick. The woman is made by God! Which is greater? The woman or the pulpit? The woman, no doubt, is the greater. The woman has more anointing than the pulpit.

Some are so religious, they have made the pulpit out of an idol god. "Do not approach, stand here, or sit there, may be the normal course for some churches today who are stricken with the plague of formalism. This is the worse kind of spiritual abuse. It says to the woman that you have *no* spiritual significance with God. You are second and lower class than the man. This lie is a deviation from the truth of the original blueprint.

***"Lo, this only have I found, that God hath made man upright; but they have sought out many inventions."*** *[Eccl. 7:29-8:1]*

God did not make her lower class or second class, but with the same quality and divine purpose as the man. She is in fact, part of the man. But the woman was created in a subordinate *position* to the man, as the body is to the head. This does not make her inferior, but part of the total equation of man. Her function and authority lies in her submission to the man, just as the body is submitted to the head. The head is not autonomous from the rest of the body, but it has the greater functions of receiving and giving command. The body cannot function without the head, neither can the head function without the body. But every part has it's own proper function, working together to reflect the image and Glory of God.

***"But I would have you know, that the head of every man is Christ; and the head of the woman is the man; and the head of Christ is God." [1 Cor. 11:3]***

***"Nevertheless neither is the man without the woman, neither the woman without the man, in the Lord. For as the woman is of the man, even so is the man also by the woman; but all things of God." [1 Cor. 11:11-12]***

Man is the head of the woman, as Christ is head of the man. Being our head, he did not make us second class, but called us to equality with Himself in every way.

*"Let this mind be in you, which was also in Christ Jesus: Who, being in the form of God, thought it not robbery to be equal with God: [Phil 2:5-7]*

*"Wherefore thou art no more a servant, but a son; and if a son, then an heir of God through Christ." [Gal. 4:7]*

*"For it became him, for whom are all things, and by whom are all things, in bringing many sons unto glory, to make the captain of their salvation perfect through sufferings. For both he that sanctifieth and they who are sanctified are all of one: for which cause he is not ashamed to call them brethren, Saying, I will declare thy name unto my brethren, in the midst of the church will I sing praise unto thee." [Heb. 2:10-12]*

*"For ye are all the children of God by faith in Christ Jesus. For as many of you as have been baptized into Christ have put on Christ. There is neither Jew nor Greek, there is neither bond nor free, there is neither male nor female: for ye are all one in Christ Jesus. And if ye be Christ's, then are ye Abraham's seed, and heirs according to the promise. [Gal. 3:26-29]*

**Submission, authority and subordination**

*"Let your women keep silence in the churches: for it is not permitted unto them to speak; but they are commanded to be under obedience, as also saith the law. And if they will learn any thing, let them ask their husbands at home: for it is a shame for women to speak in the church." [1 Cor. 14:34-35]*

*"In like manner also, that women adorn themselves in modest apparel, with shamefacedness and sobriety; not with broided hair, or gold, or pearls, or costly array, But (which becometh women professing godliness) with good works. Let the woman learn in silence with all subjection. But I suffer not a woman to teach, nor to usurp authority over the man, but to be in silence. For Adam was first formed, then Eve. And Adam was not deceived, but the woman being deceived was in the transgression." [1 Tim. 2:9-15]*

## Submission

Some men are insecure with who they are, or do not know who they are, so they are insecure and intimidated when they have a virtuous wife. They do not want her to make more money than themselves, have a degree, know more about the bible, get to much recognition in the church, or they feel less than a man or left out.

Men who are spiritually insecure, are also

unstable. They *demand submission* from their wives, but they do not submit to God. A godly woman must be subject to a godly man, both in the natural and in the spirit. If a godly woman has an ungodly man, they are unequally yoked together. She is bound, only in the natural, to submit to him, and be subordinate with all subjection, with humbleness of spirit and soundness of mind. She must love him, respect and honor him, but because the yoke is unequal, she cannot submit to him spiritually, or ask him anything concerning godly matters, because he may not know the things of God, neither have a desire to know them.

***"But the natural man receiveth not the things of the Spirit of God: for they are foolishness unto him: neither can he know them, because they are spiritually discerned." [1 Cor. 2:14]***

A man of God, however, submits to the things of God and honors Him. Therefore, a wife is subject spiritually to her husband when he is connected to God.

***"Wives, submit to your husbands as to the Lord. For the husband is the head of the wife as Christ is the head of the church, his body, of which he is the Savior. Now as the church submits to Christ, so also wives should submit to their husbands in everything." [Eph. 5:22-25]***

## Authority

### Authority is always given but never taken.

***"And Jesus came and spake unto them, saying, All power is given unto me in heaven and in earth." [Matt. 28:18]***

A godly woman never usurp, or assume authority over her husband in his position of being created first, as head of the body. However, in Christ, she have been given power and authority over the devil, who is an enemy of the head and the body.

## Usurping Authority

This has to do with attitude. **A godly woman is not dominate over the man.** If a godly woman has a husband who is a man of God, she should seek to submit to him as unto the Lord. That is not to say, that every woman who has a godly husband, do not have knowledge to share, it is a matter of attitude, and respect for authority. Submission has nothing to do with how much knowledge one may have. It has to do with obedience to God's order. A woman, no matter how virtuous, was not created to be the head of her husband, nor was the man created to be the helper of his wife, although a man should co-operate with his wife's agenda for help. He should always be ready and willing to help her in every way. Helping her is helping himself! Her agenda is to under gird the man naturally and spiritually, not to jump ahead of the man of God by leading and advising him in spiritual matters or ministry.

**A woman may gain more knowledge, than her husband, but not more spiritual authority.**

She may gain more favor and virtue with God, through faithfulness and integrity, but not enough to transform her spiritual position and promote her to head. Being more spiritual than her husband does not mean she is now qualified to be the spiritual head of the house. The position of authority is not contingent upon the achievements or abilities of the man, nor is he deemed the head because of his knowledge or his abilities. God established the man's spiritual position by creating him first. **God endowed the man with authority and dominion!**

***"But I suffer not a woman to teach, nor to usurp authority over the man, but to be in silence. For Adam was first formed, then Eve". [1 Tim. 2:12-13]***

***"For the husband is the head of the wife, even as Christ is the head of the church: and he is the saviour of the body." [ Eph. 5:23-24]***

In an army, your sergeant or lieutenant may give an order to do something, that you may know how to do better than he, but because he is the sergeant or lieutenant, you respect his authority and obey his orders.

There was a certain man who was truly anointed and ordained of God and man. He had pastored a church for a number of years. He was a young man who was very intelligent and learned in the things of God. He married a woman who also loved God, but was spiritually puffed up with pride, head knowledge, but no personal experience in ministry. She had graduated from a certified bible college, and attended a well known church in the city before she met her husband. She had the attitude of a *spiritually* dominate woman. She would not be attentive when her husband preached the word of God in a meeting, because she felt that she could say it better, or that she already knew what was being preached. He would ask her at the end of an anointed meeting, where many people were saved and delivered from various sickness and diseases, and the Word of God was preached by revelation, "Did you get anything from this service?" Her reply would be, "not really, everything you said, I already knew!" She desired to teach, but she was not teachable.

**Knowledge without wisdom is arrogance.**

*Knowledge puffeth up, but charity edifieth. [1 Cor. 8:1]*

*"The fear of the LORD is to hate evil: pride, and arrogancy, and the evil way, and the froward mouth, do I hate." [Prov. 8:13]*

**Spiritual arrogance is an abomination with God**

***"for God resisteth the proud, and giveth grace to the humble. Humble yourselves therefore under the mighty hand of God, that he may exalt you in due time:" [1 Peter 5:5-6] Therefore as the church is subject unto Christ, so let the wives be to their own husbands in every thing. [Eph. 5:24]***

**Knowledge do not equal spiritual, but submission by obedience.**

One may have much knowledge in the Word of God, but lack obedience. Life and peace follows a spiritual mind.

***For to be carnally minded is death; but to be spiritually minded is life and peace. [Rom 8:6]***

It is a shame for a haughty woman, who is puffed up with pride, whether she is learned or unlearned, to speak in the church. If she is not inspired by God through the Holy Spirit, she cannot represent His authority. She should learn by asking her husband at home. But a woman who is virtuous, has no problem with authority, submission, or humility. It is not a hard task for the virtuous woman to be virtuous. She will bsubmit to authority and be subject *first* to God, then to a godly husband. She makes intercession for her husband even if he is ungodly. She understands her function as a divine helper. [1 Sam. 25: 23-35]

## Spiritual Submission

A woman who is inspired of God has free course to speak by inspiration, the things of God, in the church, or in the city. She is led by the spirit of God to manifest His will. She submits to the order of God and the authority which God have established.

***"And the same man had four daughters, virgins, which did prophesy" [Acts 21:9]***

***"And it shall come to pass in the last days, saith God, I will pour out of my Spirit upon all flesh: and your sons and your daughters shall prophesy, and your young men shall see visions, and your old men shall dream dreams:" And on my servants and on my handmaidens I will pour out in those days of my Spirit;***

***and they shall prophesy: [Acts 2:17-19]***

God does not give the gift of prophetic utterance in vain, but He intend for it to be used by whomsoever He gives it. Whether they be male or female, adult or child. God will use whom He please for His own will and purpose. There is no difference where salvation and proclamation of the gospel is concerned.

***"For as many of you as have been baptized into Christ have put on Christ. There is neither Jew nor Greek, there is neither bond nor free, there is neither male nor female: for ye are all one in Christ Jesus. And if ye be Christ's, then are ye Abraham's seed, and heirs according to the promise." [Gal. 3:27-4:1]***

God established the order of authority beginning with Himself. He set the authority of the head and the body in place. He established everything in it's proper order. **He who is against the order, is against God!**

***"But I would have you know, that the head of every man is Christ; and the head of the woman is the man; and the head of Christ is God." [1 Cor. 11:3]***

**Ignorance is not limited to the woman.**

It is equally ashamed for a man who is arrogant and proud, whether he is learned or unlearned, but not inspired of God, to speak in the Church. **A natural, carnal minded man or woman cannot minister to a spiritual heart.** There are some men who are in the church, preaching and teaching a "*dead gospel,*" with no anointing, or inspiration from God, Perhaps because of their lack of diligence in seeking Him. They are unlearned in the things of God, and some are unsaved! Contrariwise, there are some women today that are highly anointed, humble and inspired of God. When a godly man has a virtuous wife, they flow in the harmony of the Spirit of God together. They study to compliment each other, not challenge each other. Their thoughts about God are always in agreement. The man submits to God and his wife, the woman submits to the man and God, and God honors them both.

***"Submitting yourselves one to another in the fear of God." [Eph. 5:21]***

**A man submits to his wife with love and a woman submits with honor.**

***"Nevertheless let every one of you in particular so love his wife, even as himself; and the wife see that she reverence her husband." [Eph. 5:33]***

Submission is easy to a godly woman, it is part of her character. But it is impossible for a woman of inactive, or reverse virtue. Submission is executed by faith, in obedience to humility, and the full counsel of God's Word. Do not be afraid of submission. It does not mean that you are a spiritual second class citizen, or of less importance to God. It simply mean that your function is divine and unique. No one else could do it, so God chose you! No other entity could reflect His image and likeness, like you. You are the divine reflector of glory.

**Submission is a must to the divine plan of glory. It must be activated in obedience to the Word of God.**

# Chapter Four

## Effects of the Deception

Many woman in the world have lowered their standard to become accepted in an ungodly society. So they have decided to become whatever the man wanted to use them for. Some women have been through the obstacle course and have decided to just retire from the whole idea of a relationship with men. These are just some of the effects of the deception, of the woman in the garden.

While many ungodly women have turned their desires towards other women. There are more and more young women today who have decided to choose the lesbian or gay lifestyle, because, they say, they are tired of trying to please a man. They defiantly and openly walk through the streets of the city holding hands and kissing each other, as if they were accepted of God in their abomination. Likewise many men have chosen this same ungodly lifestyle. I was recently at the mall, signing the first book that I had written, *(How To Steer Clear Of A Bozo And Stay Away From The Circus),* when a young woman came up to me and said, "I am a lesbian, and I chose this way because of all the things which I have been through with men."

***"For this cause God gave them up unto vile affections: for even their women did change the natural use into that which is against nature: And likewise also the men, leaving the natural use of the woman, burned in their lust one toward another; men with men working that which is unseemly, and receiving in themselves that recompence of their error which was meet. And even as they did not like to retain God in their knowledge, God gave them over to a reprobate mind, to do those things which are not convenient; being filled with all unrighteousness, fornication, wickedness, covetousness, maliciousness; full of envy, murder, debate, deceit, malignity; whisperers, backbiters, haters of God, despiteful, proud, boasters, inventors of evil things, disobedient to parents, Without understanding, covenantbreakers, without natural affection, implacable, unmerciful:" [Rom. 1: 26-31]***

These ungodly men and women are deceived by the enemy and are used to pervert the picture of the image and glory of God depicted in the mystery of Christ and the church.

***"Because that, when they knew God, they glorified him not as God, neither were thankful; but***

***became vain in their imaginations, and their foolish heart was darkened. Professing themselves to be wise, they became fools, And changed the glory of the uncorruptible God into an image made like to corruptible man, and to birds, and fourfooted beasts, and creeping things Wherefore God also gave them up to uncleanness through the lusts of their own hearts, to dishonour their own bodies between themselves: Who changed the truth of God into a lie, and worshipped and served the creature more than the Creator, who is blessed for ever." Amen. [Rom. 1:21-26]***

The tragic fact is that, these ungodly men and women, are in opposition to God and are snared by the devil to fulfill his will. They may think that their rebellion is justified, perhaps because they were deceived in a relationship, or perhaps they have been mentally and sexually abused as a child by a family member or others. God wants to grant them repentance from sins and heal their wounds, but they must come to Him by faith in Jesus, who is able to deliver them and cleanse them from all unrighteousness.

If you have been sexually abused or raped as a child, or otherwise, it was not your fault! Stop blaming yourself for what the devil did. If you are saved cast all your cares upon the Lord, He can handle the load of your hurts, pains and frustrations with being rejected and misunderstood. He is the only one that can deliver you.

***"Casting all your care upon him; for he careth for you." [1 Peter 5:7]***

If you are not saved, stop feeling dirty and unworthy, COME TO JESUS! You can come to Jesus by faith **right now! Don't wait!** Just stop for a minute, and pray according to the scriptures. *Pray something like this:*

FATHER I COME TO YOU RIGHT NOW, I ASK YOU TO FORGIVE ME FOR ALL MY SINS AND TRANSGRESSIONS, AGAINST YOU. I BELIEVE THAT JESUS DIED, AND THAT HE WAS BURIED, AND HE ROSE AGAIN, FOR MY SINS AND MY JUSTIFICATION. AND NOW LORD, UPON YOUR WORD , MY SOUL IS SAVED, AND MY SINS ARE FORGIVEN. THANK YOU LORD, FOR SAVING ME! IN JESUS NAME, AMEN!

***"That if thou shalt confess with thy mouth the Lord Jesus, and shalt believe in thine heart that God hath raised him from the dead, thou shalt be saved. For with the heart man believeth unto righteousness; and with the mouth confession is made unto salvation. For the scripture saith, Whosoever believeth on him shall not be ashamed." [Rom. 10:9-11]***

If you prayed this prayer from your heart, you are saved according to the Word of God. Now quickly pray and ask God to lead you to a church to receive further instructions in the Word God. Read your bible daily for nourishment. Here are a few scriptures to consider.
[Acts 2: 1-38] [Acts 1:8] [John 3:1-5]

***"But as many as received him, to them gave he power to become the sons of God, even to them that believe on his name:" [John 1: 12]***

**Welcome to the Kingdom Of God!**

# Chapter Five

## Competent and Complete

The godly woman has an endowment of virtue, *(dunamis power with God).* **She is competent and complete with all the necessary ingredients to fulfill the purpose of her creation.** This *dunamis* power was given to the woman to carry out His divine directive. This power can edify, glorify, or destroy when it is used negatively. The godly woman is virtuous because she studies to use the power given to her, for God's directive, that is, to give life more abundantly. The godly woman fears God and obeys His Word at all cost!

The godly woman studies to do good and righteous in the sight of God and man. The ungodly woman seeks whom she may devour.

In many marital relationships today, ignorance of the purpose of the woman is rampant. In today's world society, there are a number of reasons given by men for the purpose of the woman, which are all deviations from the original design. God made the original design perfect, but men have misinterpreted His plan, purpose, and image.

In our high tech world of today, men and women have undergone so many concepts, thought revisions, and differing opinions on the purposes of God's creation. Why did God create man, and why did He create woman for the man? These answers are found in His word, but they are ridiculed in today's world view.

## Happiness by Default

Many women today experience *"happiness by default!"* They may say, " oh I'm *happily married*, I've been married for twenty years." But in reality they may suffer happiness by default, that is, when the woman choose to settle for much less, and tolerate whatever comes and goes in the marriage. She may feel that the length of time for which she have been married constitutes happiness. Happiness is a byproduct. What is it that makes one happy? Many women are not happy in their marriages but they feel that they are stuck in a dead end marriage that will never change for the better, so they decide to just live with it! They are ***happy by default!*** Every marriage should be blissfully joyous, and happiness should be realized and achieved every day. The woman should never settle for thirty percent by default, because she may feel, that it is all the man is capable of putting out. Happiness can never be a goal. It can only be achieved by means of fulfillment. God wants peace and happiness in every marriage especially those who are supposed to represent Christ and the Church. Ask God to deliver you from a marriage of default, a marriage of loneliness, of physical and mental abuse, of competing with fantasies, of verbal put downs and spiritual murder! God is able to give you wisdom to make the right decisions. You will no longer be in default, Amen. You are more than what they think! You are a work of art, designed by divine craftsmanship of the master. You were filled with enough power to incite a spiritual explosion! Don't settle for status quo thinking! You are no longer in default!

**Satan wants to use every woman's power**

Although a woman may be ungodly she still have *power,* but it is used for ungodliness, for Satan's prime directive that is, to steal kill and destroy.

***"For the lips of a strange woman drop as an honeycomb, and her mouth is smoother than oil: But her end is bitter as wormwood, sharp as a twoedged sword. Her feet go down to death; her steps take hold on hell. Lest thou shouldest ponder the path of life, her ways are moveable, that thou canst not know them." [Prov. 5:3-6]***

The ungodly woman has *"dead virtue,"* because

she does not believe in Christ, therefore, her purpose is distorted and she does not know who, or what she is, so consequently, she abuse herself. So her mind is blinded by the lies told about her purpose, by the devil.

***"In whom the god of this world hath blinded the minds of them which believe not, lest the light of the glorious gospel of Christ, who is the image of God, should shine unto them." [2 Cor. 4:4]***

***"For they being ignorant of God's righteousness, and going about to establish their own righteousness, have not submitted themselves unto the righteousness of God." [Rom. 10:3]***

This ignorance is the reason why the divorce rate among Christians is the same as the divorce rate among the world, no difference! Why? Because, renovation is a process of renewing the mind, transforming the character, and mortifying the flesh. Becoming born again does not make the believer exempt from *ignorance of purpose.*

**One must seek to find, study to approve, (learn of Him) (Christ), labor to enter, mortify to be glorified, and obey the Word to transform.**

*"But we all, with open face beholding as in a glass the glory of the Lord, are changed into the same image from glory to glory, even as by the Spirit of the Lord." [2 Cor. 3:18-4:1]*

## Renewing the mind

When we come to Jesus, our spirit was redeemed and we obtain salvation, but our minds and flesh did not get "saved," nor did it instantly change. It is a process *of* ***renewing, transforming, and mortifying.***

In photography there is a process when one takes a picture on a roll of film. After the picture is taken the roll of film must be processed for development. This process of imaging is called, "C-41." This instructs the developer in what chemicals to use and how long to use it in the developing stage of the imaging process. When the C-41 process is completed the imaging process can begin. The image that is developed is the image projected onto the print.

Likewise we must go through what I call the spiritual C-41 process we will call the "R.T.M." process That is, Renewing Transforming and Mortifying.

Our minds must be renewed to function correctly in

faith, to began thinking like the original designer. Renew, means, to receive new information and discard the old. Revolution comes by revelation, and revelation is manifested by new information. The knowledge which is revealed, is new to our human nature, and it recreates what was originally intended. It brings us into faith, and knowledge of His Glory, which is right thinking with God. Which was normal before sin entered the world.

***"And have put on the new man, which is renewed in knowledge after the image of him that created him: [Col. 3:5-10]***

***"Let this mind be in you, which was also in Christ Jesus:" [Phil. 2:5]***

***Faith is correct thinking!*** Human nature inherently, has no faith in God. Renewing, puts us in position for transforming. When we are *transformed*, our mind experiences a *metamorphosis,* Revolution, or change into a new creature. The flesh (human nature) can not be *renewed or transformed*, it must *be mortified.*

We renew our minds by reading the Word of God first. Through reading or hearing the Word of God our mind is introduced to the renewing agent called faith.

*"So then faith cometh by hearing, and hearing by the word of God." [Rom 10:17]*

When we practice taking in the Word of God, it produces health and restoration to our mind, body and soul. It restores our Godlikeness!

***"Thy words were found, and I did eat them; and thy word was unto me the joy and rejoicing of mine heart: for I am called by thy name, O LORD God of hosts." [Jer. 15:16]***

Again the first step to renewal is getting the Word of God in your spirit. The second step in renewal is to ***believe what you read!*** When we believe what we hear it becomes a part of our being. It then change the course of our thinking! It brings unto righteousness.

***"For with the heart man believeth unto righteousness;" [Rom 10:10]***

The more we read and believe of the Word of God the more our mind can be renewed by the knowledge of Him. That is to conform to His image and likeness.

***"And have put on the new man, which is renewed in knowledge after the image of him that created him:" [Col. 3:10]***

***"And be renewed in the spirit of your mind;" [Eph. 4:23-24]***

## Transformation (the character)

As a caterpillar goes from being a crawling insect to a beautiful butterfly, so is everyone who is transformed by the knowledge of God. Once you have truly been transformed, you can never live like the caterpillar again.

Transformation can only take place after a renovation of the mindset, so that the spirit of man can comprehend faith. Then when faith is exercised, transformation begins. Transformation causes radical change to our character, and upgrades our value system. Continuity in faith brings continual transformation into the image of Christ, from faith to faith and from glory to glory.

***"For therein is the righteousness of God revealed from faith to faith: as it is written, The just shall live by faith." [Rom 1:17]***

***"But we all, with open face beholding as in a glass the glory of the Lord, are changed into the same image from glory to glory, even as by the Spirit of the Lord." [2 Cor 3:18]***

We must obey the Word of God to be transformed

into His image. If we obey sin, we transform into that which we obey and become a slave to it.

***"Know ye not, that to whom ye yield yourselves servants to obey, his servants ye are to whom ye obey; whether of sin unto death, or of obedience unto righteousness?" [Rom 6:16]***

***Therefore if any man be in Christ, he is a new creature: old things are passed away; behold, all things are become new. [2 Cor. 5:17-18]***

## Mind of the flesh (world system thinking)

***"And be not conformed to this world: but be ye transformed by the renewing of your mind, that ye may prove what is that good, and acceptable, and perfect, will of God." [Rom. 12:2]***

"*World system thinking,*" is thinking according to the god of this world system, Satan who is carnal, faithless, sinful, and corrupt in nature.

***"Love not the world, neither the things that are in the world. If any man love the world, the love of the Father is not in him. For all that is in the world, the lust of the flesh, and the lust of the eyes, and the pride of life, is not of the Father, but is of the world." [1 John 2:15-16]***

"*World system thinking*" cannot comprehend faith, and righteousness, just as darkness cannot comprehend light. Nor can the natural mind comprehend spiritual things, for it is foolishness to them.

***"But the natural man receiveth not the things of the Spirit of God: for they are foolishness unto him: neither can he know them, because they are spiritually discerned." [1 Cor. 2:14-15]***

**Mortification of Flesh**
**(desires of the human nature)**

***"For if ye live after the flesh, ye shall die: but if ye through the Spirit do mortify the deeds of the body, ye shall live. For as many as are led by the Spirit of God, they are the sons of God." [Rom. 8:13-14]***

The *deeds* of the body is; the working of the corrupt nature, which is *sin*. Mortification of these deeds are necessary to obtain life. It is a process of faith, patience, putting on armor, and putting off fleshly desires. Here are some of the deeds which must be put to death and eradicated.

***Mortify therefore your members which are upon the earth; fornication, uncleanness, inordinate***

*affection, evil concupiscence, and covetousness, which is idolatry: For which things' sake the wrath of God cometh on the children of disobedience: In the which ye also walked some time, when ye lived in them.*

***But now ye also put off all these; anger, wrath, malice, blasphemy, filthy communication out of your mouth. Lie not one to another, seeing that ye have put off the old man with his deeds; And have put on the new man, which is renewed in knowledge after the image of him that created him: [Col. 3:5-10***

Mortification means that we deny the flesh (or the will of the human nature) and surrender our will to the will of God!

***"and they that are Christ's have crucified the flesh with the affections and lusts." [Gal. 5:24]***

***"For which cause we faint not; but though our outward man perish, yet the inward man is renewed day by day." [2 Cor 4:16]***

The R.T.M. process must be applied first before we are then imaged in the likeness of God. To become a son of God must become subject to this process.
***If ye endure chastening, God dealeth with you as with***

*sons; for what son is he whom the father chasteneth not? But if ye be without chastisement, whereof all are partakers, then are ye bastards, and not sons. [Heb. 12:7-8]*

## Ingredients to correct thinking

*"Put on therefore, as the elect of God, holy and beloved, bowels of mercies, kindness, humbleness of mind, meekness, longsuffering;*

*Forbearing one another, and forgiving one another, if any man have a quarrel against any: even as Christ forgave you, so also do ye. And above all these things put on charity, which is the bond of perfectness. And let the peace of God rule in your hearts, to the which also ye are called in one body; and be ye thankful." [Col. 3:12-15]*

*"Forasmuch then as Christ hath suffered for us in the flesh, arm yourselves likewise with the same mind: for he that hath suffered in the flesh hath ceased from sin; That he no longer should live the rest of his time in the flesh to the lusts of men, but to the will of God.*

*For the time past of our life may suffice us to have wrought the will of the Gentiles, when we walked in lasciviousness, lusts, excess of wine, revellings, banquetings, and abominable idolatries:" [1Peter 4:1-3]*

*"Let this mind be in you, which was also in Christ Jesus: Who, being in the form of God, thought it not robbery to be equal with God: But made himself of no reputation, and took upon him the form of a servant, and was made in the likeness of men:" [Phil. 2:5-7]*

Correct thinking will insure that the marital relationship is wrought in God. When we follow the rules of correct thinking, in love, we will be successful in marriage.

***"Love is patient, love is kind. It does not envy, it does not boast, it is not proud. It is not rude, it is not self-seeking, it is not easily angered, it keeps no record of wrongs. Love does not delight in evil but rejoices with the truth. It always protects, always trusts, always hopes, always perseveres." [1 Cor. 13:4-7]***

**Spiritual abuse takes place because of wrong thinking and ignorance of the purpose of the woman.**

Remember you can do all things through Christ which strengthens you. He strengthens you in your virtue, He strengthens you in your understanding, He strengthens you in your submission, in your love of the truth, in the fellowship of His peace, and the fullness of His joy.

Remember you have a very important role in the body of Christ. You are virtuous and powerful in the sight of God! Designed with purpose and power to help! Everything you need for help is wrapped up in your virtue. The love you need is in your virtue, the financial blessings are in your virtue, your peace is in your virtue, your joy is in your virtue, your faith is in your virtue, your victory is in your virtue!

Do not practice being bitter against all the ignorant men who hurt you. You are competent and complete, a blessing to the world and gift who was not understood. With the power in you, forgive the ignorance of men and move to higher ground.

# Chapter Six

## Conforming and non-conforming virtue

***"And Samuel said, Hath the LORD as great delight in burnt offerings and sacrifices, as in obeying the voice of the LORD? Behold, to obey is better than sacrifice, and to hearken than the fat of rams. " [1 Sam. 15:22]***

Some who are professing believers in the Lord, have not obeyed the truth of the gospel, and consequently, they have become *non-conforming*. God can not use us when we do not *willfully* conform to the image of Christ through the process of obedience to His will. ***Renewing, transforming, mortification*** *and* ***discipleship.***

***"For which cause we faint not; but though our outward man perish, yet the inward man is renewed day by day." [2 Cor. 4:16-17]***

***"And he said to them all, If any man will come after me, let him deny himself, and take up his cross daily, and follow me." [Luke 9:23]***

We must, for the sake of understanding, go back to

the instructions of the designer, and re-examine the original design. Has the purpose of the design, changed from the original blueprint? Or has the material from which the design was made, become non-conformable?

***"Shall what is formed say to him who formed it, "He did not make me"? Can the pot say of the potter, "He knows nothing"? NIV [Isa. 29:16-b]***

I once worked on a job as quality control inspector. In that profession there is a standard called **"non-conforming material."** When the material used, does not conform to the intent of the designer. It may be too large or small, it may have features that the design does not call for. It may be to wide or too narrow. Whatever the discrepancy, it is then considered to be what we call **"out of tolerance."** To measure this out of tolerance condition, we use what is called a **blueprint.** This gives detail description and visual depiction of what the material is, and what it should become in the finish and final process. Since it is not possible to make non-conforming material conform to the original design, it is then good for nothing in many cases, and can only be used for **scrap.** However, some non-conforming material is **salvageable,** and must be used for something other than the original intended purpose of the designer. Or the designer can make an allowance *(tolerance)* for the non– conforming discrepancy. **"Out of tolerance,"** means that the measurement of the material is outside the scope of the designer's set parameters noted in "the print." There are only three tolerance levels in the normal print standard. **"The nominal,"** or actual tolerance. **The minimum tolerance,** and the **maximum tolerance.**

"The nominal or actual tolerance," is exactly what the material *should* become, or precisely what the designer desires of the material at the end of the process. "The minimum," is the lowest limits of what the material can be, and remain acceptable to the designer. The third level is "the maximum." This is the highest level that the material can reach and still remain acceptable to the designer. Any material that is outside of these acceptable standards are considered *"out of tolerance."* This is when the material is unacceptable to the designer, because it does not conform to his desires, and therefore it is rejected and used for scrap.

The original intention for the design and purpose of the woman has not changed. Her purpose is still the same, that is, to help the man reflect the image and likeness of God. His "blueprint," the Word of God, does not change.

***"For I am the LORD, I change not; therefore ye sons of Jacob are not consumed." [Mal. 3:6-7]***

God's purpose for the design of the woman is the same as it was in the beginning, but because sin entered the world, men and women became non-conformable and "out of tolerance." The elements of the universe fell out of harmony with the specifications of the "blue print" (the Word God) because of sin.

***"They know not, neither will they understand; they walk on in darkness: all the foundations of the earth are out of course." [Ps. 82:5-6]***

***"Behold, the LORD maketh the earth empty, and maketh it waste, and turneth it upside down, and scattereth abroad the inhabitants thereof." [Isa. 24:1]***

So, man and woman was *rejected* and driven out of the garden. Although they were non-conforming they were not yet scrap (good for nothing).

Conformance is an act of our will, or surrendering our will, to the will of God. No matter how many times I tell my wife what I desire of her, if she decides not to surrender her will, she will not conform to my desires. This submission is an act of humility and choice. Human nature was corrupted by sin and pride was woven into the fabric of our being. Surrendering our will then, is not natural or automatic. God made a plan for salvaging mankind. So that they, the material, might still be useful for His glory. He launched a long term plan for salvage of the non-conforming material. His ultimate goal was to afford an opportunity of conformance for the material, that it may be acceptable.

**Since it was, and is, impossible for God to lie, He made *promises* to the material to secure its opportunity for conformance and set in motion His plan for salvage. (or salvation)**

***"And I will establish my covenant between me and thee and thy seed after thee in their generations for an everlasting covenant, to be a God unto thee, and to thy seed after thee." [Gen. 17:5]***

Afterward He sent Moses to show the people what His tolerance levels were. The law was a *deviation* (temporary acceptability) until the specifications on the original print could be met.

***"But when the fulness of the time was come, God sent forth his Son, made of a woman, made under the law, To redeem them that were under the law, that we might receive the adoption of sons." [Gal. 4:4-5]***

Sin, had long since the garden, manifested its deadly affect on the nature of men, and had well distorted the original design for mankind. The deviation was not a change in the design nor the intention of purpose, but it was an allowance, or temporary acceptance, a new tolerance to cover the non-conformance of the material, a makeshift acceptability, until the goal of conformity could legitimately be achieved.

***"Wherefore then serveth the law? It was added because of transgressions, till the seed should come to whom the promise was made; and it was ordained by angels in the hand of a mediator." [Gal. 3:19-20]***

The nominal tolerance was to obey the law to the letter. The minimum was falling short of the nominal, but was covered under a provisionary covering written in the law. Atonement was made for the covering contained in sacrifices and offerings (grace). The maximum was the extreme limits of grace. (mercy) out of tolerance, was treading in rebellion and disobedience beyond the maximum limits. You were then, good for nothing, but scrap, wood, hay, and stubble.

***"Ye are the salt of the earth: but if the salt have lost his savour, wherewith shall it be salted? it is thenceforth good for nothing, but to be cast out, and to be trodden under foot of men." [Matt. 5:13-14]***

***"If a man abide not in me, he is cast forth as a branch, and is withered; and men gather them, and cast them into the fire, and they are burned." [John 15:6]***

Thank God for His grace and His mercy. That we were not rejected. But since He foreknew that sin would enter the world, He had already prepared our deliverance in Christ Jesus, who was slain *before* the foundation of the world. Conforming material, is material that is transformed daily, into the image Christ and likeness of God. Looking into the perfect law of liberty, the Word of God, and obeying it.

***"And we, who with unveiled faces all reflect the Lord's glory, are being transformed into his likeness with ever-increasing glory, which comes from the Lord, who is the Spirit." [2 Cor. 3:18-4:1]***

God showed us through Christ, what the original designed should have produced.

Him who is rich in mercy, pre-planned our conformation and has also made provisions for our conformity. So that, when we are conformed, we may be like Him. For the man, he is restored in dominion and authority over the earth, and into fellowship with

God. For the woman, her virtue is restored to be a divine helper of the man. Her beauty is restored, and her fellowship with God is renewed.

***"For whom he did foreknow, he also did predestinate to be conformed to the image of his Son, that he might be the firstborn among many brethren Moreover whom he did predestinate, them he also called: and whom he called, them he also justified: and whom he justified, them he also glorified." [Rom. 8:29-30]***

***"because as he is, so are we in this world." [1 John 4:17]***

**Daily may you become more and more like Him! Amen.**

# Chapter Seven

## Who Is She

**Most men in our society today do not perceive the value of the woman because they do not know what or who she is. So consequently she is abused and misused. Many times even in Christian environments the picture is distorted.**

In the beginning God made the woman from what was already created in man. He used the substance of the innermost parts of the man's being. The woman was fashioned to the perfect specifications of God's blueprint. She was an intricate part of the original *"Model T"* Adam. Designed to be a helper to the man. ***She needed no help!*** Everything that the man needed help with, was engrafted in her. **She was *his* glory.** She was made from man and was complete, with every thing to help him in every way, and without him, she had no purpose. She was exclusively created *for* the man! So then, God meticulously created every fiber of the woman, from the man, and for the man, as it hath pleased him. He created her purpose before He made her. The man Adam had to be created first, so that the woman would have a purpose. Part of that purpose was to glorify God. If a woman do not have a husband she should glorify God in her body and in her spirit. If she is married, she should reflect the glory of her husband, by *honoring* him and thus glorify God. The man should reflect the glory of God in his body and spirit. The woman can only please God in the parameters of her purpose. Outside of the designed purpose for which she was created she is dysfunctional. The woman was not created for her own agenda, or as a free agent, but for God's agenda. To help the man fulfill His plan of imaging and glory.

***"For a man indeed ought not to cover his head, forasmuch as he is the image and glory of God: but the woman is the glory of the man." For the man is not of the woman; but the woman of the man. Neither was the man created for the woman; but the woman for the man." [1 Cor. 11:7-9]***

God have placed in the woman valuable tools for life. She is a life giver as her very name implies, ***Chavvah (Eve) life-giver.***

**The woman is designed to assist in multiplying all the blessings on the earth. God told them to *multiply*, be *fruitful, subdue and replenish.***

*"And God blessed them, and God said unto them, Be fruitful, and multiply, and replenish the earth, and subdue it: and have dominion over the fish of the sea, and over the fowl of the air, and over every living thing that moveth upon the earth." [Gen. 1:28]*

## Multiply

The woman has power to help multiply. **The word *multiply* in the Hebrew is rabah (raw-baw'); meaning to increase (in whatever respect): So then God gave them the power to prosper in all things.** They were commanded to bring forth life after their kind. The power which God placed inside the woman is sufficient to multiply.

*"And Adam lived an hundred and thirty years, and begat a son in his own likeness, after his image; and called his name Seth:" [Gen. 5:3]*

## Be Fruitful

The woman has the power to ***be fruitful*** or increase in all things reflected to her, from her husband who fears the Lord, and walk in His ways.

*"Blessed are all who fear the LORD, who walk in*

***his ways. You will eat the fruit of your labor; blessings and prosperity will be yours. Your wife will be like a fruitful vine within your house; your sons will be like olive shoots around your table. Thus is the man blessed who fears the LORD" [Psa. 128:1-4] NIV***

Being fruitful has to do with increase and prosperity. The virtuous woman has the ability to take little and stretch it to meet the needs of her family.

***"She riseth also while it is yet night, and giveth meat to her household, and a portion to b: with the fruit of her hands she planteth a vineyard." [Prov. 31:15-16]***

## Replenish

Replenish, does not mean to restore the old things, but to **fill the earth,** in this instance, with new substance, new creation of life. They were instructed to reproduce and fill the earth with life more abundant.

## Subdue

The woman was to help the man subdue or bring the earth and all inhabitants in subjection. They were to have dominion over all the creation. God made the man to rule over his wife after the fall, so then, when a woman dominates a man, her actions are dysfunctional. When a man dominates his wife, he dominates his own body! When a woman dominates her husband, she is dominating her own head! **God said, subdue the earth, not each other.** However, we are to subdue the works of the flesh and the power of darkness.

***"For if ye live after the flesh, ye shall die: but if ye through the Spirit do mortify the deeds of the body, ye shall live. For as many as are led by the Spirit of God, they are the sons of God." [Rom. 8:13-14]***

Since sin entered the world, the woman's perception of her role and values were distorted, and the man's thinking became so corrupted, that God destroyed the whole world with a flood. Sin ushered in all manner of perversion and confusion.

***"And GOD saw that the wickedness of man was great in the earth, and that every imagination of the thoughts of his heart was only evil continually." [Gen. 6:5]***

**But the flood did not wash away sins.** Therefore, the same sinful nature mentality is evident today, especially in those who do not know God through the Lord Jesus Christ, who is the restorer of the breached contract between man and God.

***"For this reason Christ is the mediator of a new***

***covenant, that those who are called may receive the promised eternal inheritance-now that he has died as a ransom to set them free from the sins committed under the first covenant." [Heb. 9:15] NIV***

With all the television, cable, and internet hype, that exploits women, the moral and spiritual value of the woman has significantly diminished in our society. Because most women today do not have a clue about their *created* purpose. What *she* may think her purpose is, does not make it so. She may think highly, but live lowly. Listen to the wisdom of the Apostle Paul;

***"If the foot shall say, Because I am not the hand, I am not of the body; is it therefore not of the body? And if the ear shall say, Because I am not the eye, I am not of the body; is it therefore not of the body? If the whole body were an eye, where were the hearing? If the whole were hearing, where were the smelling? But now hath God set the members every one of them in the body, as it hath pleased him." [1 Cor. 12:15-19]***

There is a difference between the godly women and the ungodly. The godly woman have regained her power to help the man, and her virtue is restored by the Holy Spirit. Whereas, the ungodly woman have lost the power and authority spiritually to help the man.

**Sin will distort the efficacies of power and nullify authority. Sin, in essence, will rob your anointing.**

In Christ, all the components to help the man reflect the image of God, is activated in the godly, virtuous, woman. God has restored the godly woman to her rightful place in glory, that is, to be a constant blessing to the man with restored power to help multiply *(prosper)* in all things, replenish, *(to make full or complete again, as by furnishing a new supply)*, subdue, *[to bring under control]*, be fruitful, (*producing much; productive; prolific. producing results; profitable).* or having the right spiritual attitude. *She is the righteous man's glory.*

**The wicked woman can not be the righteous man's glory, nor can the righteous woman be the wicked man's glory.**

Some men have the dictatorial attitude in today's relationships which may be good in going to battle with an enemy, but it is not good for the godly woman. The godly woman has been endowed with *dunamis or virtue,* power from God, to help the man. **She has also exousia (authority to act) on her head or in her spirit which is supernatural abilities, *privilege, force, capacity, competency, delegated influence:***

**You are *Superwoman!***

That is why the woman of God is **Superwoman!** Able to go through nine months of agony and travail to bring forth life, and then be willing to have another child! **Superwoman,** she can raise the children, guide the house, wash the clothes, shop for groceries, cook the food, clean the house, and work a full time job, all in a single bound, **she is Superwoman!** A woman of God, who prays for her household, a businesswoman, an intercessor, she feeds the hungry, speaks faith to the faithless, she preaches the gospel to the humble, she is rich with the treasures of God. **She is Superwoman!** Able to nurture her children in the admonition of the Lord, Please her husband in all things. She is a blessing to the city and her virtue is present in her words. Yes, **She is Superwoman! The glory of the man, but the *power of God!***

**Superwoman,** You have supernatural abilities, privilege with God. You have power or supernatural force, you are competent and complete, intelligent and wise. You have influence to help the man in every way!

***"For this cause ought the woman to have power on her head because of the angels." [1 Cor. 11:10]***

**Power on her head means that she is connected**

**to God for the work mandated for her to do. She must receive divine instructions and revelation to help the man fulfill the will of God.**

***"In the sixth month, God sent the angel Gabriel to Nazareth, a town in Galilee, to a virgin pledged to be married to a man named Joseph, a descendant of David. The virgin's name was Mary. The angel went to her and said, "Greetings, you who are highly favored! The Lord is with you."***

***Mary was greatly troubled at his words and wondered what kind of greeting this might be. But the angel said to her, "Do not be afraid, Mary, you have found favor with God." [Luke 1:26-30]***

**Every man is blessed because of the woman whom God made for glory!**

# Chapter Eight

## The Brightness of His Glory

**When a man do not *honor* God, he can not reflect the glory of God. So when a woman do not *honor* her husband, she can not reflect his glory.**

The woman was created to be the brightness of the man's true glory, which is the glory of God. Without the glory of God, man has no glory of his own. The glory that he has, is a reflection of the glory of God.

***"Jesus answered, If I honour myself, my honour is nothing: it is my Father that honoureth me; of whom ye say, that he is your God:" [John 8:54-55]***

The word "glory" in the Greek is *DOXA, it means;* ***dignity, glory (-ious), honour, praise, worship.***

**In order for the woman to give of the light of the man's glory, he must reflect that glory (honor) to her. She can only reflect what she receives.**

***"For after this manner in the old time the holy women also, who trusted in God, adorned themselves,***

***being in subjection unto their own husbands: Even as Sara obeyed Abraham, calling him lord: whose daughters ye are, as long as ye do well, and are not afraid with any amazement.***

***Likewise, ye husbands, dwell with them according to knowledge, giving honour unto the wife, as unto the weaker vessel, and as being heirs together of the grace of life; that your prayers be not hindered." [1 Peter 3:5-7]***

*"Honor"* means that husbands should esteem highly, their wives with all their money, valuables, love, support, time, and quality attention. She should be respected highly in all things. Never talked about negatively, or put down in the company of others.

She should be the apple of the husbands eye, precious in every way, like the uncut diamond of the fortunate jeweler, so should a wife be to her husband. When a man honors his wife as an heir of the kingdom of God, God honors him and receives his prayers.

The Greek word for ***honour*** here, is **Time, (tee-may) it means; a value, i.e. money paid, or (concretely and collectively) valuables; by analogy, esteem (especially of the highest degree), or the dignity itself:**

When a man reflects God's glory to the woman, he will seek ways to please her, he will honor her in the natural, as well as in the spirit. His focus is twofold, the one on the Lord, and the other on his wife.

***"An unmarried man is concerned about the Lord's affairs-how he can please the Lord. But a married man is concerned about the affairs of this world-how he can please his wife- and his interests are divided. An unmarried woman or virgin is concerned about the Lord's affairs: Her aim is to be devoted to the Lord in both body and spirit. But a married woman is concerned about the affairs of this world-how she can please her husband." [1 Cor. 7:32-34] NIV***

Reflecting God's glory means that all that God honors man with, it is in essence, reflected to the woman for the imaging process to be fulfilled in the man. The man is said to be the image and glory of God. The woman, who is the intricate component of the man, helps him achieve that image and glory by submission and reflection. She is designed to reflect what is given to man of God.

**She incubate, analyze, magnify, and multiply what is given to her of man.**

The same way a magnifying glass works by reflection and magnifies what is reflected through it, so is the woman who receives reflection from God through the man. She magnifies his power! She is also an anointed incubator of glory. She will sometimes store up a man's good reflection and shun the negative reflection. It may take some time for her to store up enough glory to lift the man to honor if he is in fact dishonorable. She will incubate little glory at a time as she receives it from God, through the man. She is a divine helper of man.

## Incubate

A woman is a divine incubator of glory. She incubates whatever the man gives her. If a man gives a seed, she will incubate it and give him a child, give her and idea, she incubate it, and will make it work. Give her a word she will incubate it!

***"And when they had seen it, they made known abroad the saying which was told them concerning this child."***

***"And all they that heard it wondered at those things which were told them by the shepherds. But Mary kept all these things, and pondered them in her heart." [Luke 2:17-19]***

## Analyze

**The woman analyze everything she hear and see and make her decisions based upon her analysis.**

***"And when the woman saw that the tree was good for food, and that it was pleasant to the eyes, and a tree to be desired to make one wise, she took of the fruit thereof, and did eat, and gave also unto her husband with her; and he did eat." [Gen. 3:6]***

***"And Sarai said unto Abram, Behold now, the LORD hath restrained me from bearing: I pray thee, go in unto my maid; it may be that I may obtain children by her. And Abram hearkened to the voice of Sarai. And Sarai Abram's wife took Hagar her maid the Egyptian, after Abram had dwelt ten years in the land of Canaan, and gave her to her husband Abram to be his wife." [Gen. 16:2-4]***

## Multiply

The woman not only multiply in childbearing, but also in blessings, and prosperity. She is able to take a little money and stretch it to purchase all the necessities of the house with change left over. She was designed to prosper.

***"The heart of her husband doth safely trust in her, so that he shall have no need of spoil. She considereth a***

*field, and buyeth it: with the fruit of her hands she planteth a vineyard. She girdeth her loins with strength, and strengtheneth her arms. She perceiveth that her merchandise is good: her candle goeth not out by night." [Prov. 31:11] [Prov. 31:16-18]*

## Magnify

**The woman glorify God when she magnify what she has received in her spirit.**

*"And Mary said, My soul doth magnify the Lord, And my spirit hath rejoiced in God my Saviour." [Luke 1:46-48]*

**When the helper, helps the man to reflect the image and likeness of God, He is glorified.**

**The helper must have more *power in her function,* than the helpee.** She do not need help or permission from the man, to be his helper! She have a mandate from God, engrafted in her very being, *to help.*

Likewise when a man's car breakdown with a flat tire, he cannot lift the car by brut strength, so he incorporates some help, "the jack." The jack has hydraulic power that can lift the car with all of its baggage in the trunk, with ease and speed. The jack is happy to lift the car, because that's why it was designed. It do not mind getting a little dirty or getting underneath the car, because in doing so, it fulfills it's purpose for existing. However, no matter how powerful the jack is, it cannot function as a tire. Likewise the woman has power from God to help the man through her "*virtue power.*" But she can only function with her anointing in the parameters of her virtue. She cannot become a "front tire!" She can only do the things which brings glory to God by faith. It is easy and spiritually normal for the woman to be able to help the man. She not only help the man individually, but mankind. A woman who is godly, will find herself helping others, feeding the hungry, and ministering to the needs of the people, because the Holy Spirit, who is our helper lives inside her and ignites her mandated function to help. She cannot help it, she must help!

When a woman has a husband who happens to be unsaved or unbelieving, she must use her virtue for sanctification to cover him. She will go to great lengths to protect him by intercession.

***"And fell at his feet, and said, Upon me, my lord, upon me let this iniquity be: and let thine handmaid, I pray thee, speak in thine audience, and hear the words of thine handmaid.***

*Let not my lord, I pray thee, regard this man of Belial, even Nabal: for as his name is, so is he; Nabal is his name, and folly is with him: but I thine handmaid saw not the young men of my lord, whom thou didst send" [1 Sam 25:24-25]*

*"For the unbelieving husband is sanctified by the wife, and the unbelieving wife is sanctified by the husband: else were your children unclean; but now are they holy." [1 Cor. 7:14]*

**When a godly woman has an ungodly husband she will love him by faith and help him by virtue.**

# Chapter Nine

## Beauty To Behold

***"And I John saw the holy city, new Jerusalem, coming down from God out of heaven, prepared as a bride adorned for her husband." [Rev. 20:14]***

The woman was designed for a man's love. Sexuality from the man is a necessary component for fulfillment of that love. A women then must receive love for fulfillment. That is why Satan has exploited and distorted the picture by confusing sex with love. So many young women of all cultures today are seduced with all types of sexual perversion, lesbian, gay lifestyle, polygamy, orgies, pornography, and all such like things. Some women who experienced a bad relationship, have decided to just stay single with a nasty attitude towards *all* men! It is an abomination to God, because the picture it illustrates is a perversion of the truth. Christ and His wife, the Church.

The scripture say that marriage describes a picture of Christ and the church. So when a man or woman violate their sexuality in this way, they make God a liar!

*"Who changed the truth of God into a lie, and worshipped and served the creature more than the Creator, who is blessed for ever. Amen. "For this cause God gave them up unto vile affections: for even their women did change the natural use into that which is against nature:" [Rom. 1:25-26]*

A man who *is saved* must practice discipline to mortify the ungodly desires of the flesh. His desires sexually, should be only towards his wife. He should seek to give his wife *due benevolence.*

***"Let the husband render unto the wife due benevolence: and likewise also the wife unto the husband." [1 Cor. 7:3-4]***

Due benevolence means that a man is indebted to love his wife and to fulfill her desires for love. Likewise she is indebted to honor him as she honors God!

***"Husbands, love your wives, even as Christ also loved the church, and gave himself for it; This is a great mystery: but I speak concerning Christ and the church." [Eph. 5:25]***

***"Nevertheless let every one of you in particular so love his wife even as himself; and the wife see that she reverence her husband." [Eph. 5:32-6:1]***

If temptation tries to enter, *resist the devil, and he will flee.* The man must command obedience from his flesh. Not according to the flesh, or natural thinking, but according to the mind of Christ. He must learn to shun the very presence of evil. To set yourself in agreement with Christ, is an act of *your* will. It is not automatic. Therefore, a man cannot simply say, in a sexual crisis, "what would Christ do?" Jesus did not have a wife after the flesh, but after the spirit, nor did He express His sexuality in the flesh, but in the spirit. HIS WIFE IS THE CHURCH! Jesus' expression of love and devotion to the church is our example of the love and devotion a man should attain with His wife. Jesus honored His wife with all of His valuables, and recognized her glory and beauty.

***"And I John saw the holy city, new Jerusalem, coming down from God out of heaven, prepared as a bride adorned for her husband." [Rev 20:14]***

He gave her all that he had. He restored to her eternal life that was originally given and lost in the garden, as a gift to her because he loved her. He gave her apostles, and prophets, evangelist, pastors and teachers for her edifying. Their intimacy and love produced many children after their kind, and thus we are called the children of God.

***"For it became him, for whom are all things, and by whom are all things, in bringing many sons unto glory, to make the captain of their salvation perfect through sufferings." [Heb. 2:10]***

Jesus loved His wife so much, that He was not only *willing* to die for her, but when the time came to prove it, He did! A man then must have a relationship with the invisible God, ***Lord Jesus Christ***, to understand the principles of love towards his wife. Then he must set himself in agreement with the Word of God by way of covenant with God in obedience to holiness.

***"I made a covenant with mine eyes; why then should I think upon a maid?" [Job 31:1]***

## Making covenant gives purpose to discipline

A man then must strive to achieve his maximum sexuality with his wife. This is not an automatic act of plain human nature. Any animal can have sex, but not intimacy. The need for a wife's sexual fulfillment should NEVER go undone! Neither should the man look for others to fulfill his sexual desires.

***"The husband should fulfill his marital duty to his***

***wife, and likewise the wife to her husband. The wife's body does not belong to her alone but also to her husband. In the same way, the husband's body does not belong to him alone but also to his wife. Do not deprive each other except by mutual consent and for a time, so that you may devote yourselves to prayer. Then come together again so that Satan will not tempt you because of your lack of self-control." [1 Cor. 7:3-5]***

The woman should always be an embodiment of his desires and the man should always be the woman's anticipation for love. Her very speech should arouse his sexuality. He should always be intrigued with her love. His exploration should be for HER satisfaction, and when a man satisfies his wife, he satisfies himself. Her presence should satisfy his eyes, and her laughter should be his joy.

***"Let thy fountain be blessed: and rejoice with the wife of thy youth. Let her be as the loving hind and pleasant roe; let her breasts satisfy thee at all times; and be thou ravished always with her love. And why wilt thou, my son, be ravished with a strange woman, and embrace the bosom of a stranger? For the ways of man are before the eyes of the LORD, and he pondereth all his goings." [Prov. 5:18-21]***

A woman can only help in the parameters of her anointing. She cannot help the man in doing the things which only he was designed to do. She cannot make her husband obey God!

**Cheating on a spouse is like cheating on God!**

***"But whoso committeth adultery with a woman lacketh understanding: he that doeth it destroyeth his own soul." [Prov. 6:32]***

***"You ask, "Why?" It is because the LORD is acting as the witness between you and the wife of your youth, because you have broken faith with her, though she is your partner, the wife of your marriage covenant." [Mal 2:14-15] NIV***

BROTHERS AND SISTERS MAKE UP YOUR MINDS **BEFORE** YOU GET MARRIED, TO BE FAITHFUL TO YOUR WIFE OR HUSBAND. IF YOU CANNOT BE FAITHFUL DON'T GET MARRIED!

# Chapter Ten

## The Virtuous Woman

### *Prov. 31: 10-31*

***"Who can find a virtuous woman? for her price is far above rubies."***

A virtuous woman is a woman of *power with God.* The Hebrew word for *virtue* is ***Chayil*****, It means strength, might, efficiency, wealth, strength, ability, efficiency, wealth, force, an army.**

This word *Chayil* is the equivalent of the Greek word *Dunamis.* When a women is virtuous she is connected to God in a supernatural way. God's virtue answer's her faith. Her faith reflects that virtue to her husband first. Then all whom she may come in contact with, experience the light of her reflected power. A woman filled with the Spirit of God, strives to walk in the virtue of the Holy Spirit. She is not haughty in her spirit. For Jesus said, ***learn of me for I am meek and lowly of heart.*** She is not a loud stubborn woman, because the scripture says, that **the virtuous woman has a meek and quiet spirit.** Not always negatively talking and babbling about others, and their business.

Her time is spent blessing her God with the fruit of her lips and her husband is blessed by her presence. She guides the house with wisdom.

***"She seeketh wool, and flax, and worketh willingly with her hands."***

**The virtuous woman is not lazy.** She will work willingly. Her husband does not have to beg for her help. She knows what her house needs and strategically work out plans to achieve her goals to help. The virtuous woman is a worker of good things, and does not mind hard work.

***"She is like the merchants' ships; she bringeth her food from afar."***

**The virtuous woman is meticulous about what she feeds her family.** She receives revelation from God and feeds her family spiritual food from on high. She receives the hidden manna and prepares a feast for her family.

***"She riseth also while it is yet night, and giveth meat to her household, and a portion to her maidens."***

**The virtuous woman do not mind waking up late at night to hear from God.** She shares her knowledge with her household. She will intercede when everyone else is asleep. She will pray to God when no one else is around to hear it. Her meat is spiritual sustenance for a spiritual household.

***"She considereth a field, and buyeth it: with the fruit of her hands she planteth a vineyard."***

**The virtuous woman is a business woman,** always finding the best deals. She is prosperous in all that she set her hands to do. She recognize her portion of the vineyard, and ministers in the field for harvest. She is a seed planter, and saving souls is her business.

***"She girdeth her loins with strength, and strengtheneth her arms."***

**The virtuous woman is girded about with joy in the Lord, which is her strength.** She strengthen her arms by building up herself on her most holy faith praying in the Holy ghost. She is girded about with truth and the fruit of the Spirit.

***"She perceiveth that her merchandise is good: her candle goeth not out by night."***

The virtuous woman knows her own anointing, and she is not wavering in her abilities to believe and trust

God. When darkness come around, her light does not go out through unbelief, but she lets her light shine before men that they may see her good works.

***"She layeth her hands to the spindle, and her hands hold the distaff."***

**The virtuous woman is a worker in the spirit.** She will fast and pray *before* problems arise. She is skillful in spiritual warfare.

***"She stretcheth out her hand to the poor; yea, she reacheth forth her hands to the needy."***

**The virtuous woman is a giver of good things.** She has good hospitality and knows how to entertain angels. She will feed those who are hungry with the Word of God. She will cloth those who are spiritually naked with the Word of God, and those who have natural needs she will give natural clothing. She will heal those who are sick with the Word of God. She will visit those in prison with the assurance and comfort of the Word of God. She is compassionate to those less fortunate.

***"She is not afraid of the snow for her household: for all her household are clothed with scarlet. She maketh herself coverings of tapestry; her clothing is silk and purple."***

**The virtuous woman is prosperous in everything she set her hands upon. She multiplies her blessings and give of her substance to her family, so that all in her house are recipients of her blessings and virtue.**

She is clothed with a robe of righteousness and her house is blessed with the garments of salvation.

*"I put on righteousness, and it clothed me: my judgment was as a robe and a diadem. I was eyes to the blind, and feet was I to the lame. I was a father to the poor: and the cause which I knew not I searched out." [Job 29:14-16]*

***"Her husband is known in the gates, when he sitteth among the elders of the land."***

The virtuous woman seeks opportunity to magnify the name of her husband, she speak highly of him at all times, as unto the Lord. She do not compete with his leadership, and dishonor him by questioning his authority or challenging him in the company of others.

***"For after this manner in the old time the holy women also, who trusted in God, adorned themselves, being in subjection unto their own husbands: Even as Sara obeyed Abraham, calling him lord: whose***

***daughters ye are, as long as ye do well, and are not afraid with any amazement." [1 Peter 3:5-6]***

***"She maketh fine linen, and selleth it; and delivereth girdles unto the merchant."***

***"Strength and honour are her clothing; and she shall rejoice in time to come."***

**The virtuous woman is strengthened by the Word of God,** and gives glory and honor to God through her praise and worship. She rejoice in the Lord always.

*"Rejoice in the LORD, you who are righteous, and praise his holy name." [Ps. 97:12-98] NIV*

***"She openeth her mouth with wisdom; and in her tongue is the law of kindness."***

**The virtuous woman is a pioneer of seeking out the deep things of God,** so that when she speaks, it is as the oracle of God. The virtuous woman has power in her tongue, she is able to speak life into any situation. Her words penetrate the walls of hell. She snatches souls out of darkness and usher them into light. Her words are mixed with *dunimis* power and faith, to heal the sick and raise the dead! Because of her words, many are healed and delivered. She is kind in all that she does, and with her mouth she have built the city.

***"She looketh well to the ways of her household, and eateth not the bread of idleness. Her children arise up, and call her blessed; her husband also, and he praiseth her."***

**The virtuous woman prays for the deliverance of her household. The ways of her household are ordered by the Lord.**

Her husband and her children are blessed by her, she is the pillar of truth and the bond of the family.

***"Many daughters have done virtuously, but thou excellest them all. Favour is deceitful, and beauty is vain: but a woman that feareth the LORD, she shall be praised."***

**A virtuous woman fears the Lord and departs from evil. God honors the virtuous woman with grace and blessings.**

***"Give her of the fruit of her hands; and let her own works praise her in the gates." [Prov. 31: 10-31]***

This is a picture of the virtuous woman who loves the things of God, and fears the Lord. She is a woman of integrity, honor and respect. Her strength is in her love of God, and she honors him with glory, by submission and honor to her husband.

## Healing Virtue

**The woman has healing virtue in her. It is what allows her to comfort, to build up, to edify, to please, to restore and to heal the sick. This *dunamis* power of healing is manifested in the virtuous woman. Sometimes just a touch or a word from a virtuous woman is all a man need for healing.**

***"And Jesus said, Somebody hath touched me: for I perceive that virtue is gone out of me. And when the woman saw that she was not hid, she came trembling, and falling down before him, she declared unto him before all the people for what cause she had touched him and how she was healed immediately." [Luke 8:46-47]***

Jesus had both virtue, dominion, and authority, because He is the second Adam with no sin. Just as God gave the earth to His first created son, Adam, He also Gave to His only begotten Son Jesus the second Adam.

***"For God so loved the world, that he gave his only begotten Son, that whosoever believeth in him should not perish, but have everlasting life." [John 3:16]***

# Chapter Eleven

## The Virgin and The Wife

***"There is a difference also between a wife and a virgin. The unmarried woman careth for the things of the Lord, that she may be holy both in body and in spirit: but she that is married careth for the things of the world, how she may please her husband." [1Cor. 7:34]***

In our society, we are infiltrated with so much ungodliness and perversion of the truth, that young women have serious struggles with the peer pressures of being a virgin. There are suggestions in every area of our lives that fornication is acceptable behavior. The world has portrayed the picture of the so called "normal family," which may engage in fornication and or adultery.

The television programming today is full of lust, and images of lewdness, and fornication. But a young woman should remain a virgin until she is ready to be given in marriage. It is a blessing when a young woman decides to remain a virgin, and keep herself without blemish and holy before God, until she is married. The virgin represents the church, pure, untainted with sin, without spot or blemish. When she is finally married, the marriage itself is a spiritual covenant made between the man, the virgin and God. The man promises to love, cherish and honor the virgin all the days of his life until death. The woman makes the same promises. A young woman who remains a virgin until marriage, is virtuous and have place with God. When a man finds a *virtuous* woman, he obtains favor of the Lord, because a virtuous woman has power with God. The covenant between a man and a virgin must be confirmed by blood, when the marriage is consummated.

That is why, when the marriage is finally consummated and the virgin is penetrated, her seal is broken in her virginity and the marriage is consummated with her blood, and the covenant is cut. The shedding of the blood represents the cutting of a covenant or agreement.

***"Yet ye say, Wherefore? Because the LORD hath been witness between thee and the wife of thy youth, against whom thou hast dealt treacherously: yet is she thy companion, and the wife of thy covenant." [Mal 2:14]***

The picture of the virgin is a glorious picture of Christ and the church.

***"For I am jealous over you with godly jealousy: for I have espoused you to one husband, that I may present you as a chaste virgin to Christ. [2 Cor. 11:2-3]***

**The covenant was cut between Christ and His wife at the cross of Calvary, by blood.**

***"But one of the soldiers with a spear pierced his side, and forthwith came there out blood and water." [John 19:34]***

***Now the God of peace, that brought again from the dead our Lord Jesus, that great shepherd of the sheep, through the blood of the everlasting covenant, Make you perfect in every good work to do his will, working in you that which is wellpleasing in his sight, through Jesus Christ; to whom be glory for ever and ever. Amen." [Heb. 13:20-21]***

## The Virgin

To the young women who are virgins consider what I say. Keep yourself Holy and without blemish until you are blessed by God in marriage. Don't worry, love will not pass you by! You will have power with God, and He will give you the desires of your heart, when you take your virginity seriously by surrendering your body and spirit to God. Do not allow the devil to steal this precious gift from you through fornication and sin. Be faithful in your virginity and God will bless you in your marriage. Your husband will be honored by your presence and your children will be like a fruitful vine.

Your body is for the Lord Jesus, and you are espoused to one husband.

***"Know ye not that your bodies are the members of Christ? shall I then take the members of Christ, and make them the members of an harlot? God forbid. What? know ye not that he which is joined to an harlot is one body? for two, saith he, shall be one flesh. But he that is joined unto the Lord is one spirit. Flee fornication."***

***"Every sin that a man doeth is without the body; but he that commiteth fornication sinneth against his own body. What? know ye not that your body is the temple of the Holy Ghost which is in you, which ye have of God, and ye are not your own? For ye are bought with a price: therefore glorify God in your body, and in your spirit, which are God's." [1 Cor. 6:15-20]***

Do not allow the pressure of the world to seduce you. Remember the devil wants to steal your inheritance and your reward. Having a sexual relationship before marriage is a distortion and a perversion of the spiritual picture of Christ and the church. So for the virgin, she is blessed of God as long as she is faithful. She is blessed of God also when she is finally married. Perhaps you were an adulterous, fornicator, before you got saved, and now you have come to God by way of Jesus Christ. In the spirit you are no longer a fornicator and an adulterer, but a chaste virgin! You are brand new in the sight of God. If you are a women of virtue, and you have guilt concerning your past relationships, and bad decisions, ask God to for give you and then you must forgive yourself! You are a new creature in Christ. You are a spiritual virgin!

***Therefore if any man be in Christ, he is a new creature: old things are passed away; behold, all things are become new.2 Cor 5:17***

***"As far as the east is from the west, so far hath he removed our transgressions from us." [Ps. 103:12]***

***"And their sins and iniquities will I remember no more." [Heb. 10:17]***

## The virtuous wife

When the woman becomes a wife, her role is towards her husband and towards God. She helps him in bringing God honor and glory.

***"A virtuous woman is a crown to her husband: but she that maketh ashamed is as rottenness in his bones." [Prov. 12:4]***

***"but she that is married careth for the things of the***

***world, how she may please her husband." [1Cor. 7:34]***

***"Wives, submit yourselves unto your own husbands, as unto the Lord. For the husband is the head of the wife, even as Christ is the head of the church: and he is the saviour of the body. Therefore as the church is subject unto Christ, so let the wives be to their own husbands in every thing." [Eph. 5:23-24]***

***"Nevertheless let every one of you in particular so love his wife even as himself; and the wife see that she reverence her husband." [Eph. 5 :28]***

The virtuous wife walks by faith, and confidence in the Word of God. She submits to the love of her husband with all willfulness and humility. God listens to her intercession, and answers her cries for help in fulfilling His will in her *to help.*

**Only God can teach a man how to love his wife**

***"Husbands, love your wives, even as Christ also loved the church, and gave himself for it;" [Eph. 5:26]***

God knows how to deliver the virtuous woman's husband from the clutches of the enemy, and give her the victory when she makes request and petitions to him. She is the apple of His eye, and anointed to help fulfill the will and purpose of God. A virtuous wife has favor with God concerning her husband. She has power over his body, to help the man surrender to glory. Just as the man should surrender to God's glory, so should the woman surrender to the glory reflected from God through the man. She should compliment his glory, bless his blessings, anoint his anointing, agree with his spirit, and be subject in his kingdom willfully, knowing that the kingdom is also her inheritance. He cannot be king with out his body. A head without the body is dead!

## Husbands Love Your wives

1. NEVER: should your wife compete with your friends for your time and attention. Give her the first fruits of your time. Loving her is a *spiritual* thing!

   ***"So ought men to love their wives as their own bodies. He that loveth his wife loveth himself." [Eph. 5:28-29]***

2. NEVER: neglect your wife's need for affection and romance! Give her love and she will give you honor.

   ***"Let the husband render unto the wife due benevolence: and likewise also the wife unto the husband." [1 Cor.7:3]***

3. NEVER: play mind games with your wife, it is like

playing a chess game against yourself, YOU WILL LOSE in the end!

***"Nevertheless let every one of you in particular so love his wife even as himself; and the wife see that she reverence her husband." [Eph. 5:33]***

4. NEVER: plant rotten seeds for a fruitful harvest. What you say, and how you say it, will be recorded. She will incubate, analyze, multiply, and magnify! "***Husbands, love your wives, and be not bitter against them." [Col. 3:19]***

5. NEVER: place your job, business, church, pastor, doctor, lawyer, friends, teacher, children, mother or father, above your wife!

***"For this cause shall a man leave his father and mother, and shall be joined unto his wife, and they two shall be one flesh." [Eph. 5:31]***

6. NEVER: complement other women more than you do your wife. She is *your* glory!

***"For a man indeed ought not to cover his head, forasmuch as he is the image and glory of God: but the woman is the glory of the man." [1 Cor. 11:7]***

7. NEVER: forget to celebrate your love for your wife

every chance you get. Birthdays, anniversaries, and special occasions.

8. NEVER: Allow your wife to be overburdened with a full time job, attending to the children, cleaning the house, washing the cloths, shopping for groceries, and stroking *your* ego, without lifting a finger to help her!

***"And the LORD God said, It is not good that the man should be alone; I will make him an help meet for him." [Gen. 2:18]***

The helper is in need of co-operation and assistance for the effectiveness of divine help!

***"She also rises while it is yet night, And provides food for her household, And a portion for HER MAIDSERVANTS." [Prov. 31:15] NKJV***

9. NEVER: show a lack of support for your wife's interests. If she wants to shop, say yes, if she want to start a business say yes, if she wants to go on a trip, say yes, just say yes, yes, yes, and you will not go unrewarded!

10. NEVER: rebuke your wife or discuss personal matters in the face your friends, mother, father or children.

11. NEVER: expect your wife to respond without preparation! Always take time for ROMANCE!!!!

12. NEVER: hinder your wife from worshipping and praising God! She could be your only lifeline! Do not take away her liberty in the Lord!

13. NEVER: be inconsiderate in allowing her time for HERSELF! Allow her room to breathe!

***"House and riches are the inheritance of fathers and a prudent wife is from the LORD. [Prov. 19:14]***

## Wives Love your husbands

1. NEVER: dishonor or disrespect your husband, no matter what he does or says, he belongs to God!

***"Therefore as the church is subject unto Christ, so let the wives be to their own husbands in every thing." [Eph. 5:24]***

2. NEVER: usurp or assume command of authority, because *you* think he's not doing an adequate job!

***"But I suffer not a woman to teach, nor to usurp authority over the man, but to be in silence." [1 Tim. 2:12]***

3. NEVER: tear down your husband's character to others by revealing all his business to family, friends, mother, father, sisters, brothers, pastors, teachers, and strangers.

"***He that covereth a transgression seeketh love; but he that repeateth a matter separateth very friends." [Prov. 17:9-10]***

***"If you argue your case with a neighbor, do not betray another man's confidence, or he who hears it may shame you and you will never lose your bad reputation." [Prov. 25:9-10] NIV***

4. NEVER: publicly embarrass or humiliate your husband, or show a lack of concern for his honor before others.

***"A virtuous woman is a crown to her husband: but she that***

***maketh ashamed is as rottenness in his bones" [Prov. 12:4]***

NEVER: Reflect a lie! If he honors you, and love you, reflect that love and honor back to him, multiplied! She who refuses to reflect the love and honor given by her husband is a liar!

***"A gracious woman retaineth honour:" [Prov 11:6]***

6. NEVER: seek counseling from your children, concerning your husband's problems!

***"Counsel is mine, and sound wisdom: I am understanding; I have strength." [Prov 8:14]***

7. NEVER: expect your husband to somehow automatically know what you are thinking, or what you want, he cannot read your mind! Communicate by words easily understood.

8. NEVER: neglect your husband's need for affection and intimacy. Never use sex as an embargo or bargaining chip.

***"Defraud ye not one the other, except it be with consent for a time, that ye may give yourselves to fasting and prayer; and come together again, that Satan tempt you not for your incontinency." [1 Cor 7:5-6]***

9. NEVER: stop praying for your husband to be the man

of God that he was called to be! If you want him to become as Abraham, then you must become as Sarah.

***"Even as Sara obeyed Abraham, calling him lord: whose daughters ye are, as long as ye do well, and are not afraid with any amazement." [1 Peter 3:6]***

10. NEVER: tear down your husband's ego by speaking insults and showing lack of confidence in him.

***"Every wise woman buildeth her house: but the foolish plucketh it down with her hands." [Prov. 14:1]***

11. NEVER: compare or expect your husband to have another man's anointing. He is like no one else!

12. NEVER: practice lying to husband, for, or about, money, stealing from him is like stealing from yourself!

***"For the love of money is the root of all evil: which while some coveted after, they have erred from the faith, and pierced themselves through with many sorrows." [1 Tim. 6:10]***

13. NEVER: fill your house with contention and arguing, but strive to keep peace in the presence of the Lord!

***"A continual dropping in a very rainy day and a contentious woman are alike." [Prov. 27:15]***

# Chapter Twelve

## What's in a Bone

In the spirit, the woman is bone of the man, or body of the man, just as the church is bone of His bone, and the body of Christ. So the way a man treats his own body, he ought to treat his wife. When a man commit the act of fornication, he sins against his wife, who is, in the spirit, his own body, flesh of his flesh, and bone of his bone. Even if he is not married, his wife (rib) is *inside* of him, in the spirit. When a woman commit fornication, she sins against her head, even if she is not yet married, she is engaged to Christ. Who is the head of the body.

***"Flee fornication. Every sin that a man doeth is without the body; but he that commiteth fornication sinneth against his own body." [1 Cor. 6:18]***

The woman is the eyes, ears, nose, feet, the hands, the function and the directive of the man's glory and honor. The man is the head of his wife by virtue of chronology and divine order. His primary, divine, function is to glorify God.

***"I have glorified thee on the earth: I have finished***

***the work which thou gavest me to do." [John 17:4-5]***

As head of his wife, he is to receive divine instructions to cultivate her in bringing glory to God. When a man loves his wife, he glorifies God.

**When a woman over rules her husband she dishonors God.**

Just as the body cannot proceed without the head, neither should a wife proceed without her husband's leading. *Only in the Lord.* When a woman is bitter and angry against her husband, or a husband against his wife, they cannot reflect the glory of God.

***"Wives, submit yourselves unto your own husbands, as it is fit in the Lord. Husbands, love your wives, and be not bitter against them." [Col. 3:18-19]***

***"Likewise, ye husbands, dwell with them according to knowledge, GIVING HONOUR UNTO THE WIFE, as unto the weaker vessel, and as being heirs together of the grace of life; that your prayers be not hindered." [1 Peter 3:7]***

If you want to be blessed, you must follow the rules for glory. For the man, you must submit to God in all things, and praise God without wrath and bitterness towards your wife. You must walk by faith. Give love and honor to your wife. Subdue *all* works of the flesh, daily. God made the man to be his image and glory. A representative of Him on earth. You are perfected in Christ to reveal His glory.

***"That the name of our Lord Jesus Christ may be glorified in you, and ye in him, according to the grace of our God and the Lord Jesus Christ." [2 Thess. 1:12]***

A man then, must walk in representation of his Lord and not in his own will. When a man honors his wife, he reflect the glory of God to her by surrendering his authority in the area of her function, allowing her to function as his help in bringing glory to God. When the woman moves in her function as the divine help, she multiply the honor back to her husband through surrendering her authority to him in all things. She will respect him, submit to his vision and help fulfill his agenda. She will reverence him, by acknowledging his position of authority with God. When a man surrenders his authority and dominion to God by honoring his wife as the divine helper or weaker vessel, and the wife multiply the honor to her husband, God is glorified. He looks at them as one body. Then the body becomes a living sacrifice, holy acceptable unto God.

***"beseech you therefore, brethren, by the mercies***

***of God, that ye present your bodies a living sacrifice, holy, acceptable unto God, which is your reasonable service." [Rom. 12:1]***

If there is no honor, there is no glory. Presenting yourself before God, means that honor is being reflected. When Adam and Eve lost their glory through sin and shame, they could no longer honor God, so they could no longer present themselves before God, because they had a stinking sacrifice, unacceptable to God.

***"And they heard the voice of the LORD God walking in the garden in the cool of the day: and Adam and his wife hid themselves from the presence of the LORD God amongst the trees of the garden. And the LORD God called unto Adam, and said unto him, Where art thou? And he said, I heard thy voice in the garden, and I was afraid, because I was naked; and I hid myself."[ Gen. 3:8-10]***

When there is no honor, sin lies at the door, and the sacrifice is unacceptable.

***"A son honoureth his father, and a servant his master: if then I be a father, where is mine honour? and if I be a master, where is my fear? saith the LORD of hosts unto you, O priests, that despise my name.***

*And ye say, Wherein have we despised thy name?"*

***"Ye offer polluted bread upon mine altar; and ye say, Wherein have we polluted thee? In that ye say, The table of the LORD is contemptible. And if ye offer the blind for sacrifice, is it not evil? and if ye offer the lame and sick, is it not evil? offer it now unto thy governor; will he be pleased with thee, or accept thy person? saith the LORD of hosts."*** *[Mal. 1:6-8]*

God is then glorified by honor. A man must obey God, and honor his wife who is his body, with all his love, respect, friendship, quality time, money, and everything he owns, even his very life! The woman likewise must reflect this honor in obedience to God and by reverencing her husband in all things, surrendering her authority to him as unto the Lord, even as the Church is surrendered unto Christ. Then this honor is presented before God as a living sacrifice, even as our Lord Jesus has shown us to do.

***"Therefore as the church is subject unto Christ, so let the wives be to their own husbands in every thing. Husbands, love your wives, even as Christ also loved the church, and gave himself for it; That he might sanctify and cleanse it with the washing of water by the word,***

***That he might present it to himself a glorious church, not having spot, or wrinkle, or any such thing; but that it should be holy and without blemish." [Eph. 5:24-27]***

Just as Christ loved his wife, He gave every man the perfect example of how to love his wife, by presenting her *(the body),* to God without spot, or dishonor, a living sacrifice, holy and acceptable.

**She is bone of your bone.**
**Love her and she will honor you!**

***"For we are members of his body, of his flesh, and of his bones. For this cause shall a man leave his father and mother, and shall be joined unto his wife, and they two shall be one flesh." [Eph. 5:30-31]***

It is the man's responsibility to humble himself and seek the face of God, through denying ungodliness and the lust of this world. Prayer and fellowship with God is the key ingredient in obedience to His Word. We must study the Word of God daily, for strength in our spiritual lives. We need the nourishment from the Word to sustain us spiritually, just as we need natural food for the nourishment of our natural bodies.

There is a natural body and a spiritual body. God is

the sustainer of both the natural and the spiritual. He purposed everything to be beautiful in His own time.

***"He hath made every thing beautiful in his time:" [Eccl. 3:7]***

***Whoso findeth a wife findeth a good thing, and obtaineth favour of the LORD. [Prov. 18:22]***

When we understand the divine plan of the creation and manifestation of the woman, we can say, like God, **"It is Very Good!"**

# Chapter Thirteen

## Women of Virtue

**Eve**—Life giver— Gen. 3:20

**Sarah—** obedient to her husband— 1 Pet. 3: 6

**Zappora–** Moses' wife —-wise—Exo. 4:24-25

**Bathsheba**—stolen virtue —2 Sam. 2:5

**King Lamuel Mother–** virtuous— Prov. 31

**Rahab** —–feared the God of Israel— Josh. 2:3-4

**Abigail**-wisdom— beauty—intelligence -1 Sam 25:3

**Deborah**— reluctant strategic leader — Judges 8:9-10

**Candace–** Queen— Acts 8: 27

**Pontius pilate's wife**– recognized righteousness-Matt. 29: 19

**Elizabeth**– mother of the prophet— Luke 1:1-13

**Esther—**virtuous and courageous—Est. 4:16

**Eunice**– Timothy's mother— faithful –2 Tim. 1:5

**Hagar**—substitute of promise— Gen. 16: 1

**Gomer-wife of Hosea -** prostitute-abused virtue-Hos. 1:2

**Herodius Daughter**—virtue misused virtue—Mark 6: 22-24

**Delilah**—virtue used in reverse— Judges 16:6

**Jezebel**— reverse virtue— 1 Kings 21:7-10

**Vashti—**beautiful but rebellious and disobedient —— reverse virtue—Est. 1:12-13

**Leah --wife of Jacob**— fruitful — Gen. 30:17-21

**Mary Martha** — friends of Jesus—Matt. 10: 38-42

**Mary mother of Jesus**– Obedient -virtuous-John 2:5

**Miriam** — the Prophetess —Exo. 15:20

**Ruth**— humble and virtuous— Ruth 3: 9 –11

**Susanna**— a giver and minister of righteousness —Lk. 8-3

**Magdalene**—Restored virtue—Luke 8: 2-3

**Pricilla** — Minister of the gospel ——Rom. 16:3

***"Many daughters have done virtuously, but thou excellest them all." [Prov. 31:29]***

Thank God for all the virtuous women of today, whom, in these last days, may have suffered many things at the hands of the enemy through ignorant vessels of dishonor. You have a great cloud of witnesses from virtuous women of old.

You are women of honor, who have their testimonies of faith, endurance, prayer and fasting, of suffering and pain, of disappointments and heartbreak, of gaining loved ones and losing them, of warfare and strategies, of healings and miracles, of casting out demons and rejoicing in the Lord. Women of today, you are the anointed generation of virtue whom God have chosen to be conformed to His image. That He may show forth His power and His glory through you, that He may present you faultless before His presence with exceeding joy. Not having spots (besetting sins) or blemishes (works of the flesh) or any such thing. Without blame in a world full of contradiction of all righteousness. But you are the virtue (light) of the world, and the reflector of His glory. Your Husband is He who created all things and beings. Who delivered you from unreasonable men, and brought you forth as pure gold. **Brothers be warned, you are God's representative on earth, you must treat the woman RIGHT!**

***"For thy Maker is thine husband; the LORD of hosts is his name; and thy Redeemer the Holy One of Israel; The God of the whole earth shall he be called.***

***For the LORD hath called thee as a woman forsaken and grieved in spirit, and a wife of youth, when thou wast refused, saith thy God." [Isa. 54:5-7]***

May God add to your faith, virtue, according to the (*dunimis)* power of His might, which He, so richly gave us through the knowledge of His glory, by Jesus Christ our Lord. Who have given us all things.

***"According as his divine power hath given unto us all things that pertain unto life and godliness, through the knowledge of him that hath called us to glory and virtue:" [2 Pet. 2:3]***

**Restoration of Glory**

***"And it shall come to pass in the last days, saith God, I will pour out of my Spirit upon all flesh: and your sons and YOUR DAUGHTERS SHALL PROPHESY, and your young men shall see visions, and your old men shall dream dreams: And on my servants and ON MY HANDMAIDENS I WILL POUR OUT IN THOSE DAYS OF MY SPIRIT; and they shall prophesy:" [Acts 2:17-18]***

God has restored through the Lord Jesus Christ, the virtue, (*divine power to help)* to the woman and the exousia (*authority to have dominion of the earth)* to the man through pouring out His Spirit on *all* who believe.

The woman is restored to full power in glory, and the man to honor and fellowship with God.

May today's woman of virtue and honor, be blessed with the fruit of righteousness, and that your words continue to heal the people in your path. You are not *every woman,* you are a virtuous woman! Working with a divine plan, powerfully anointed and appointed for such a time as this!

YOU ARE THE VICTORY!

## Where is my Glory?

The character of the godly woman is as a priceless pearl, not to be traded for anything, because she is more than what one could imagine. She is the godly man's glory.

**"Have you seen my glory?"** She is wonderful, and precious, more desirable to me than rubies, diamonds, gold, silver, or all the things, which a man could possess. Nothing can compare to her!

She is awesome! My heart races with excitement, and I am weak in my knees when I am in her presence. Her beauty absorbs me, and I meditate on her loveliness day and night. Her skin is fine as silk, soft and smooth. Her hair is as the waves of the sea in all its' splendor and glory. Her eyes are clean and wide with anticipation, for she trusts in my strong arms for protection, but she knows my strength comes from the Lord. Her face is narrow, and her mouth is of few words.

A meek and quiet spirit she has, because she fears the Lord, the Most High God. Her voice is pleasant to my ears, that I am an eager listener. She always speaks positive things to my spirit, that I am confident and edified by her love. Yea, she speaks of me in the gates of the city, as if I were some great king from a far country. The people honor me because of her speech. In all her prayers she vows to do me good, and not evil all the days of her life. Her love for me is overwhelming, that I securely trust in her. She is highly intelligent, because she trusts in the Lord. She is a businesswoman also, always producing new keys to prosperity, that I have no need of material things.

She is a skilled thinker, a professional in her craft. Her virtue is powerful and her anointing covers my heart. She loves knowledge and wisdom; they are the tools of her profession. She is rich with the treasures of God; even her children are attentive to her words. **Have you seen my glory?**

She is my lawyer in my defense, always covering even my transgressions with the fragrance of her love. ***[Prov. 17:9]*** When I am sick, she is my doctor, by way of intercession to the Most High God, for my deliverance. She prepares my food with tender love, that my health is speedily recovered. With her kiss, she assures my heart, that I am safely in love. "**My wife is awesome!**"

# Behold The Woman

If this book has been a blessing to you, please feel free to e-mail us at the address listed below, or write us at:

Anointed Publishing
2940 W. Lincoln Ave. # D410
Anaheim Ca. 92801

To order other books written by Apostle Wayne Wallace see the available books list and select the books you desire, use the order form on the following pages.

**We pray that every soul that read this book have new found honor and love for God's gift to man, "The Woman." And that every woman understand how to reflect honor and respect by love to the man.**

Our e-mail address is: sonsofgod3@juno.com

Phone: (562) 918-0950

Visit our website at:

www.deeperrevelation.org